L'Chayim - To Life

Memoirs of a Survivor
of a Nazi Ghetto

By Lisa E. Mishler
Prose by Rabbi Stephanie S. Aaron

L'Chayim - To Life

Memoirs of a Survivor of a Nazi Ghetto, a Partisan and Russian Soldier in World War II

Acknowledgments:
With special thanks to Rabbi Stephanie S. Aaron, whose encouragement led to the undertaking of this huge and highly emotional project. Her beautifully written prose enhanced every aspect of this work. I would also like to thank my husband Charles for his continued support of my endeavors. My daughter Stephanie contributed to the commentary of which I am very grateful. A special thanks to Stacey Lane for her technical/design support and being available all hours of the day and to Janet Rhoades for proofreading and editing.

Lisa Mishler

I was asked by Rabbi Stephanie Aaron to paint this body of work in remembrance of the Holocaust. I am a local artist as well as the daughter of Holocaust survivors and heroes Sol and Luba Kotz. Throughout my adult life I have heard many of the stories narrated in my father's memoirs. More recently, as I read his recounting of events and did some of my own research, I experienced an emotional journey which inspired the paintings presented in this book.

One night I had a dream. It was deep, dark and eerie. The thoughts and images continued throughout my waking hours. I painted "Rise of the Forgotten". As I painted I felt as though I was honoring the souls of those murdered in the holocaust.

Lisa Mishler

Rise of the Forgotten

Tallis, prayer shawl, you envelop and hold. Reb Zalman, Z"l, taught that when we grasp our tsitsit, our knotted fringes, we fly to the sacred ground. Where do we make our sacred ground now? The ground is ruptured, scattered with remains of our shuls, burnt fragments of scrolls swirl over our heads. We hold onto our tsitsit demanding sacred ground; we will not let go of who we are. We are defined by Torah which yields a world of purpose and meaning. We cannot; we do not; we will not bind ourselves to a world of hatred and destruction. We carry our vision of this other world with us wherever we go. Tallis, prayer shawl, you envelop and hold.

Rabbi Stephanie S. Aaron

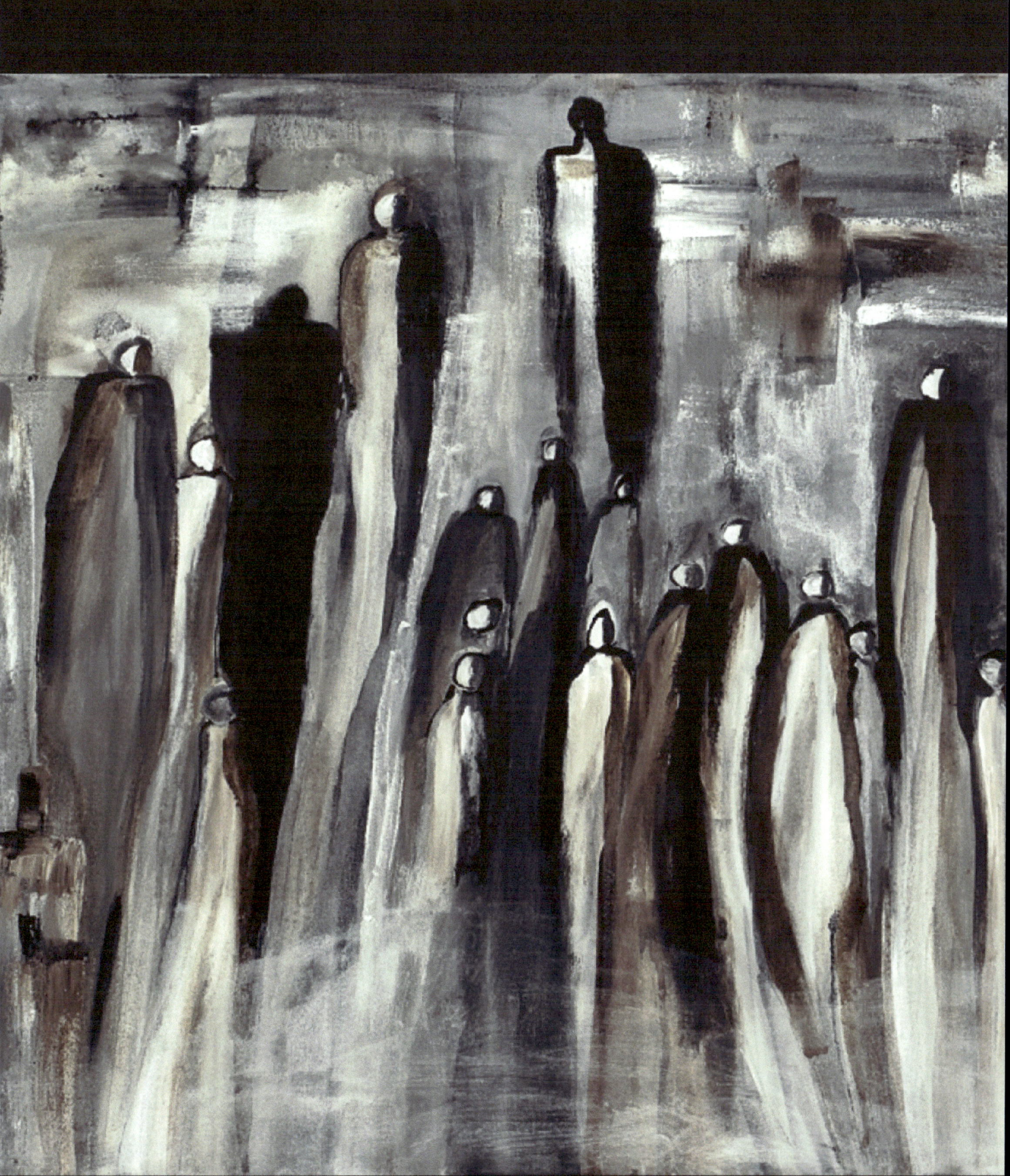

Innocence of Shabbas

This image represents the naivety of the people of Europe thinking that they were safe from the Nazis.

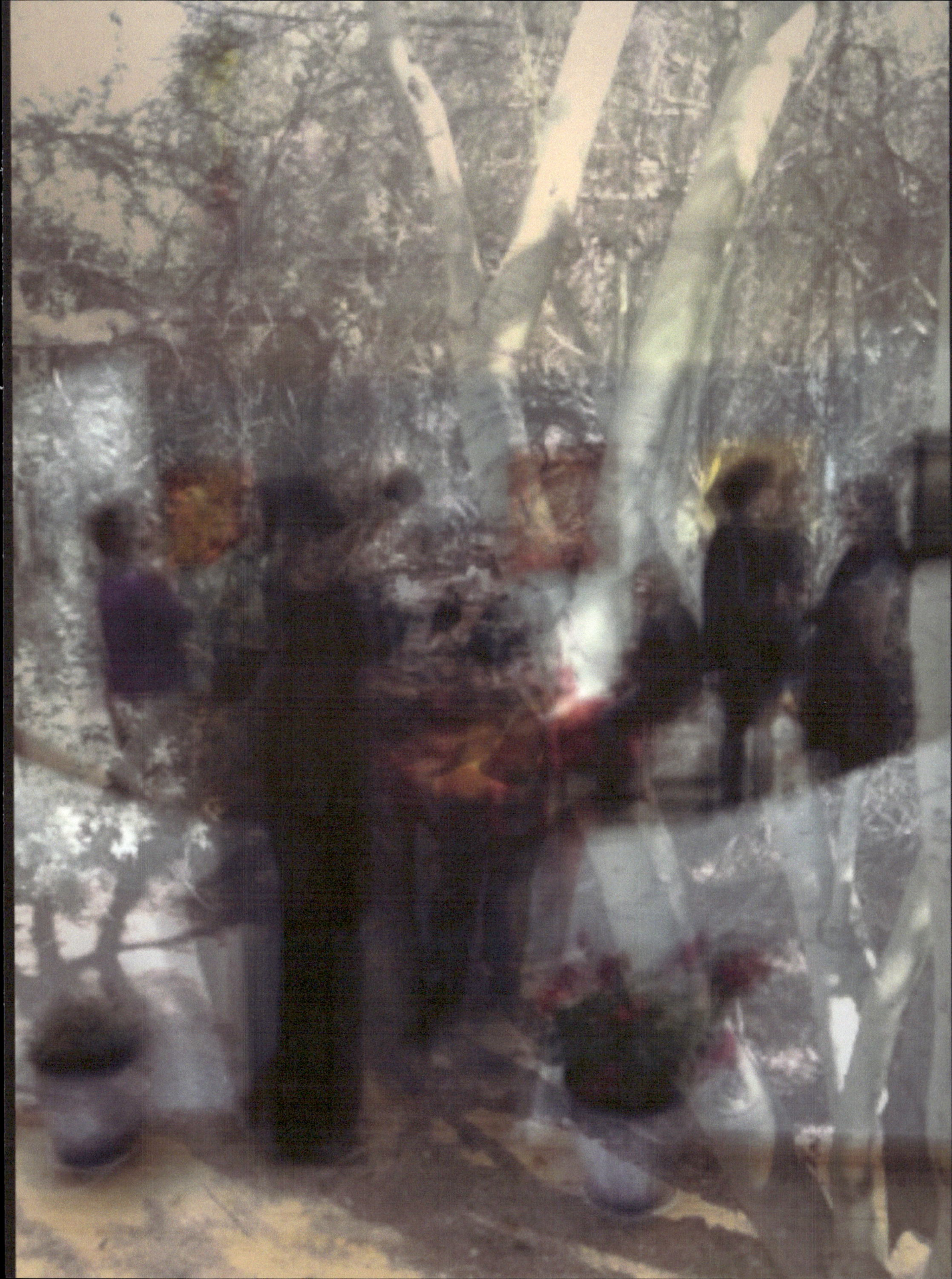

Sol Kotz

Sol Kotz was born Zalman Ber Kotz August 13, 1921 in Glubokoye, Poland and died November 8, 1994 in Tucson, Arizona.

Sol and Luba, his wife, overcame incredible odds as heroes and survivors of the Holocaust. Sol and Luba served together in the Partisan Army. Sol went on to serve as an officer in the Russian Army. He came to the United States October 29th, 1946 with Luba to escape persecution and start a new life.

With artistic talent, a good head for business and design, Sol prospered as a self-made businessman in the United States. Although he was strong-willed and often stubborn, Sol was charismatic and had a twinkle in his eye. His laugh came from deep within. He had a presence you could not ignore.

Sol was generous and donated to charities. He made it a priority to give to the Jewish Community and Israel. He was a co-founder of the first synagogue in Scottsdale, Arizona. Sol could be heard saying "If you're not giving until it hurts, you're not giving".

Sol had a deep love for his children and grandchildren. They, in turn, loved and admired him. His daughter Lisa recollects him telling her to never give up, to hold her head up high and to be proud of who she is. These words are fitting coming from a survivor of the unimaginable circumstances of the Holocaust.

Luba Kotz

Luba was born April 27, 1921 in Vilna Poland and passed April 19,1972 in Tucson, Arizona. Luba was wonderful with poetry and language. She spoke seven different languages fluently.

During the years of 1943-1945 Luba fought with the Partisan army, she served as a nurse and a soldier. She was in charge of smuggling Jewish orphans out of war zones.

After the death of her first born (Efryim) during the World War II, Luba often stated how blessed she felt to be able to come to America have three more children. She gave unconditional love to them and her two grandchildren. Luba was a strong woman and strong willed. She was honest and devoted to her family.

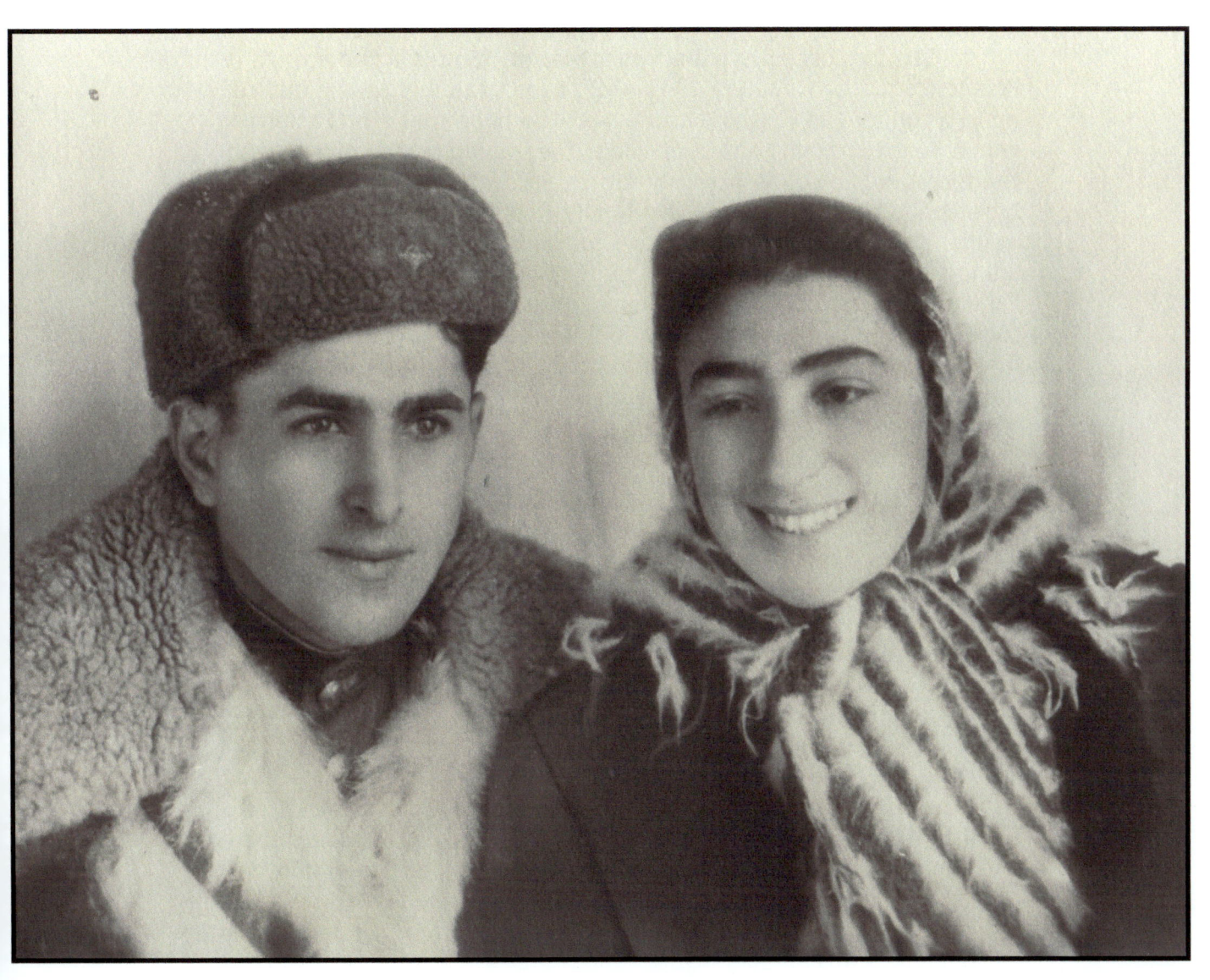

Zalmon and Luba Kotz

Luba's Journey

The Germans occupied Vilna which was my mother's home town in Poland from approximately 1942-1945. Luba's family fled the city to make a run for the Russian border, with the hope that the Russians would fight to regain control of Vilna. They found refuge in a cave in the forest outside of Polutsk. My father, Sol, wanted to continue on to his home in Glubokoye where his family was, but could not convince my mother's father to go. My mother Luba wanted to stay with her family. Sol left for Glubokoye in October of 1941 and arrived January 5, 1942. My mother eventually followed, leaving her family behind in the cave. It took her three months to travel 120 miles to Glubokoye. (She found out later that shortly after she left her family, they had been shot and killed in the cave.)

Excerpt from Sol's Memoirs

"She was walking slowly and wearily toward me dressed in sheep's wool boots covered by rubber galoshes, lined with a heavy felt of sheep-skin. Her hands were wrapped warmly in her woolen gloves and her head and face were covered by a heavy woolen shawl. Over this she wore the white-sheet covering of the Ski-Trooper, used for concealment in the snow. She had used this in the forest when she had been forced to sleep in the deep drifts."

"Luba made an incredible journey on foot, from the forest in and around Polutsk, in the dead of winter, to Glubokoye. That she traveled one hundred and twenty miles, through deep snow drifts and frozen roads, with little or nothing to eat to sustain her will always be a source of wonder to me. That she was able to survive those forty below zero temperatures was miraculous."

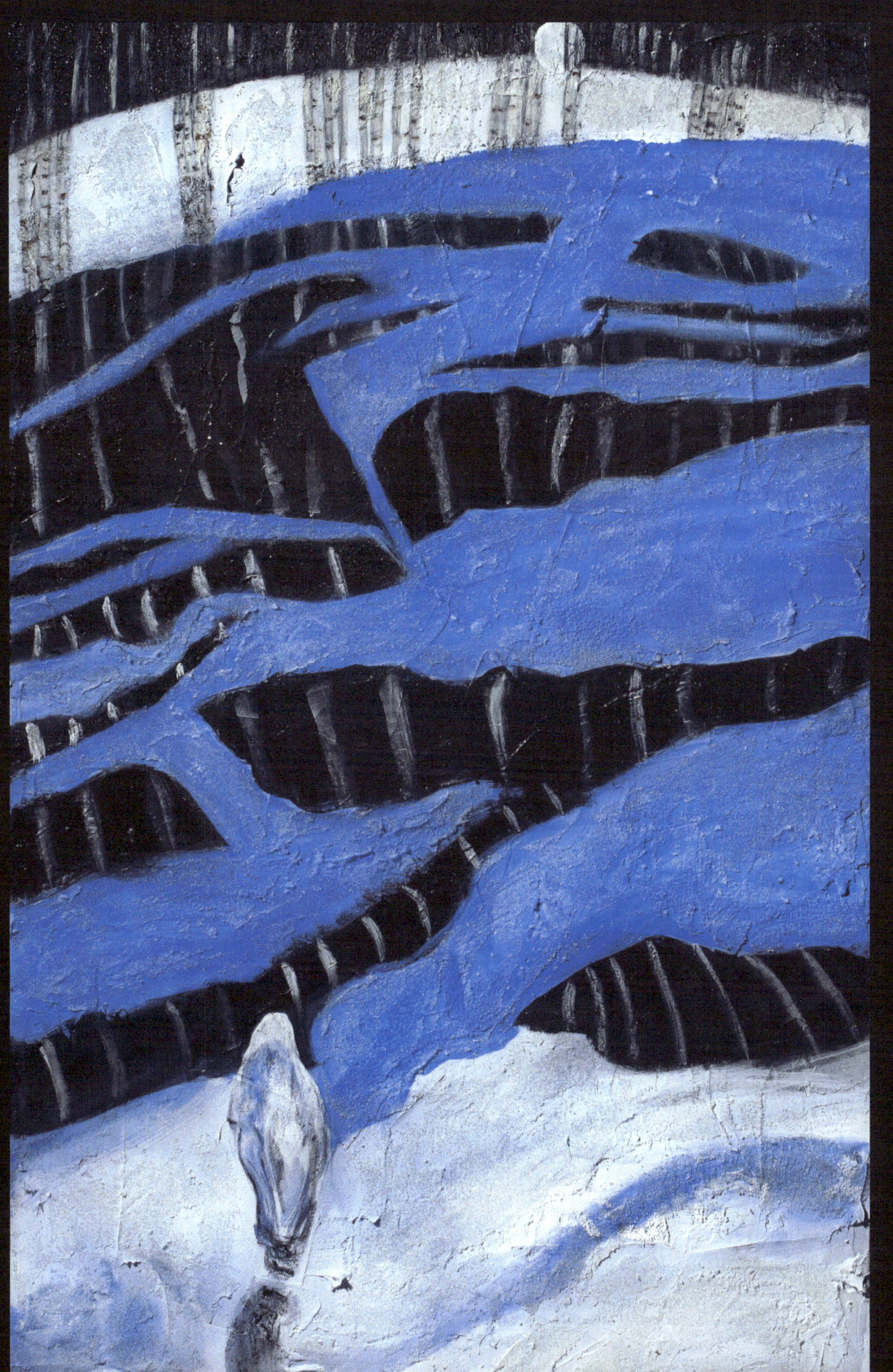

March of the Children

Luba walked with the children, leading them to where the Jews were camped in the woods. Each of them an orphan; each of their parents murdered by the Germans. The children were silent points of light; each one carried within Nitsot Elohai, sparks of G-d's light. That night, they were protected; the gun was silent; they passed by the Germans.

Mr. Frost, in 1923 from a safe and distant shore, you paused in your woods, explaining, "The woods are lovely, dark, and deep, but I have promises to keep, and miles to go before I sleep, and miles to go before I sleep".* What safe place could you or any of us ever hope to have when Jewish children slip past Nazi patrols whose sole aim is to murder them? Your woods were lovely, dark and deep; their woods were treacherous, dangerous, and deep. Yet, that night they had promises to keep, they had miles to go before they could sleep. Luba brought them safely into the Partisan camp.

Rabbi Stephanie S. Aaron

*Exerpt from Robert Frost's "Stopping by Wood on a Snowy Evening". Copyright 1923

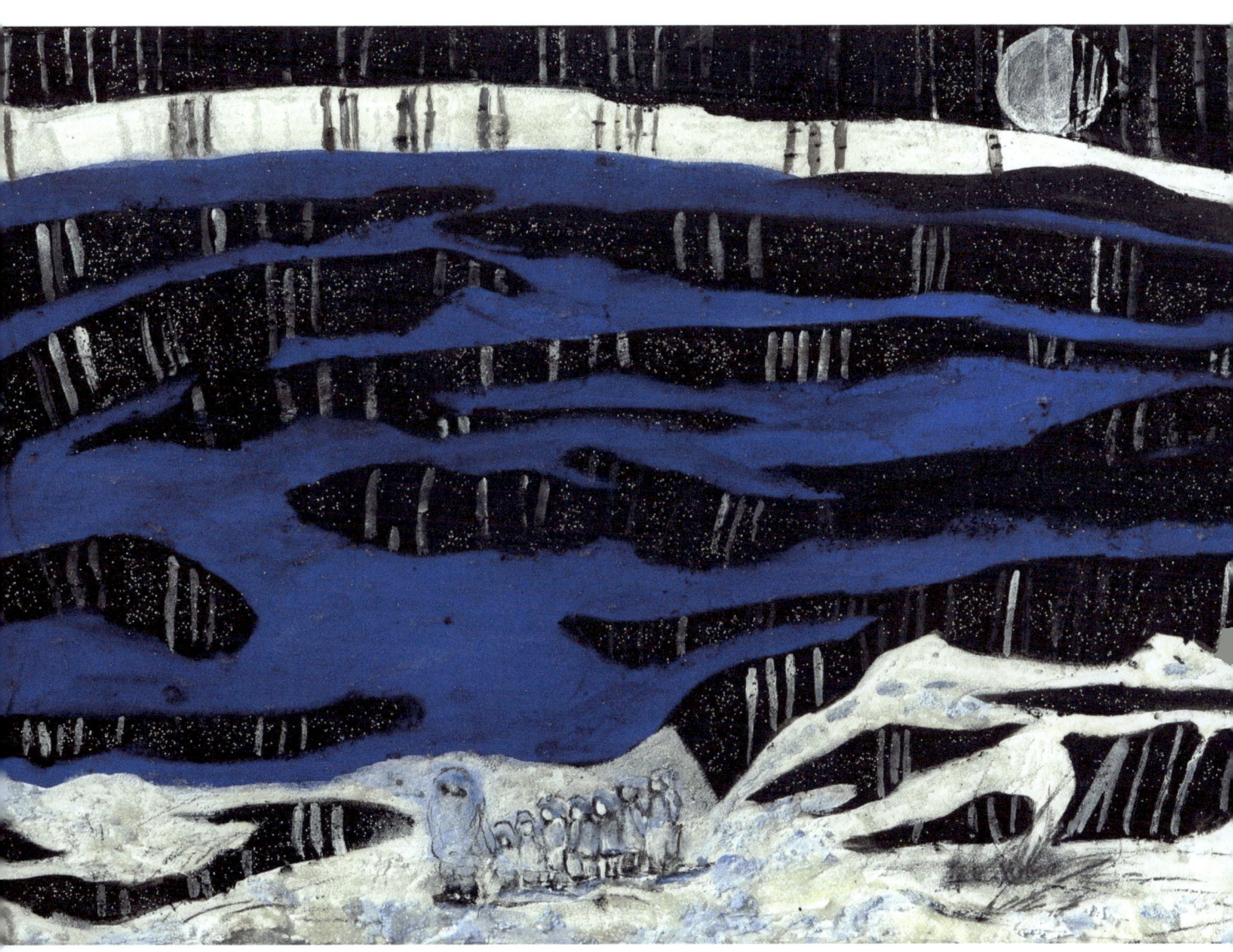

Always With Me

"Always"
"There are many with me." Psalm 55:19

And who are they? They are the angels who watch over people. Rabbi Yehoshua ben levi said: an entourage of angels always walks in front of people, with the angels calling out. And what do they say? "Make way for the image of the Holy One, Blessed be G-d."

Deuteronomy Rabba, Re'eh 4

What happens in a world where the job of the angels becomes too huge, too overwhelming? Where the world is a chaos of shouts of evil men and the silence of the men who do not raise a fist, a question, even a whimper against them? Where by-standers grab what they can in haste from the homes of their Jewish neighbors and then stand and watch those same Jewish neighbors be dragged into the woods to be shot, thrown into their burning synagogues, or shoved onto waiting trains. What happens when the voices of the angels are overpowered by the screams of Jewish children as they are ripped from the sheltering arms of their parents?

Can we still sense these holy beings and their holy message? Luba could; Luba did. Always; her angel was always with her; constantly strengthening her for her journey forward. Urging her over the frozen ground; growing her courage as she helped the children grapple with snow and hatred, hunger and despair. Luba and her angel making their way in a world that was in a frenzy of Nazi rage against her people and the angels that walked before them.

Rabbi Stephanie S. Aaron

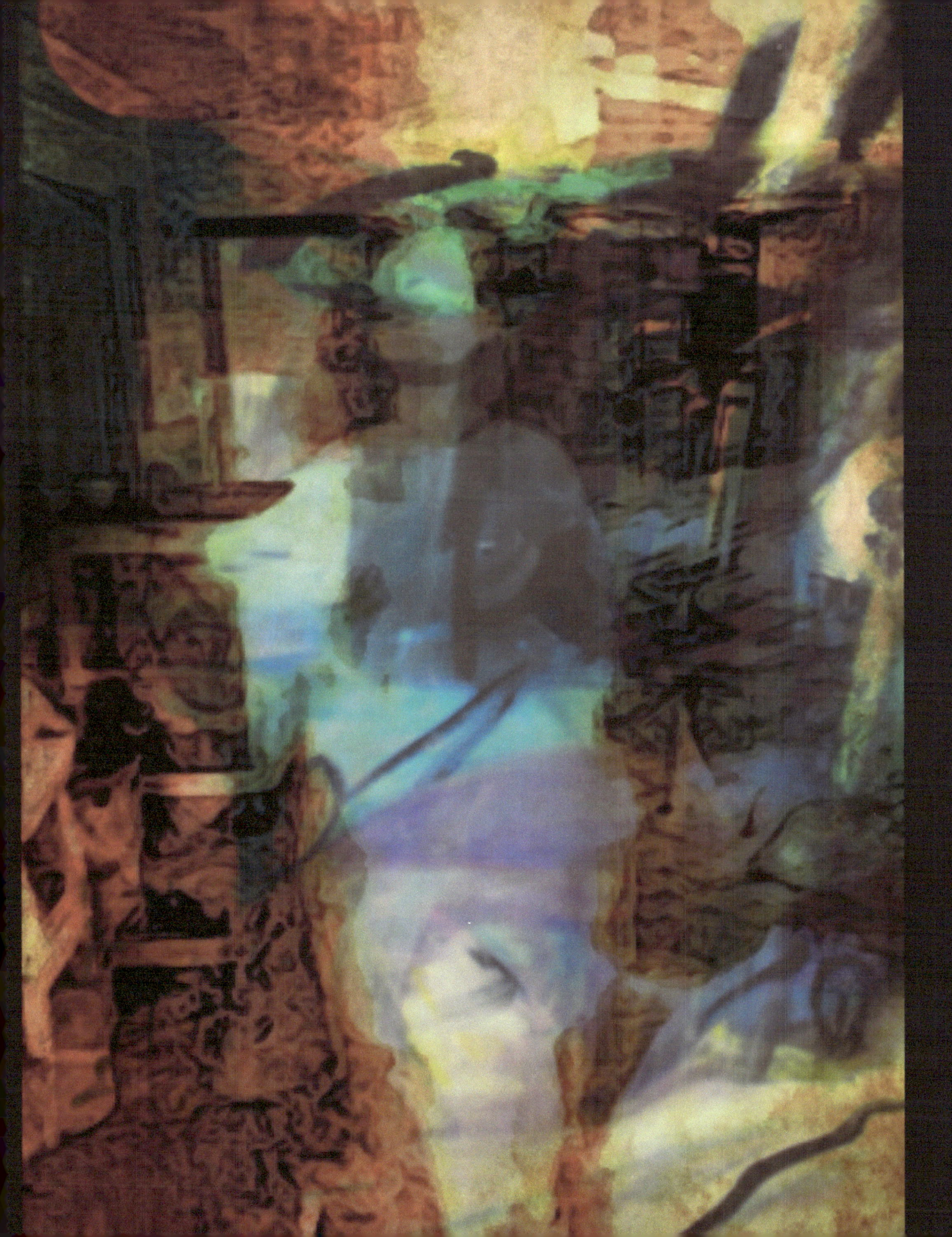

IN A MOMENT

In a moment your life can change. What once was, is no longer. Life, death, birth, sickness and just pure chance can change your life, all in a moment.

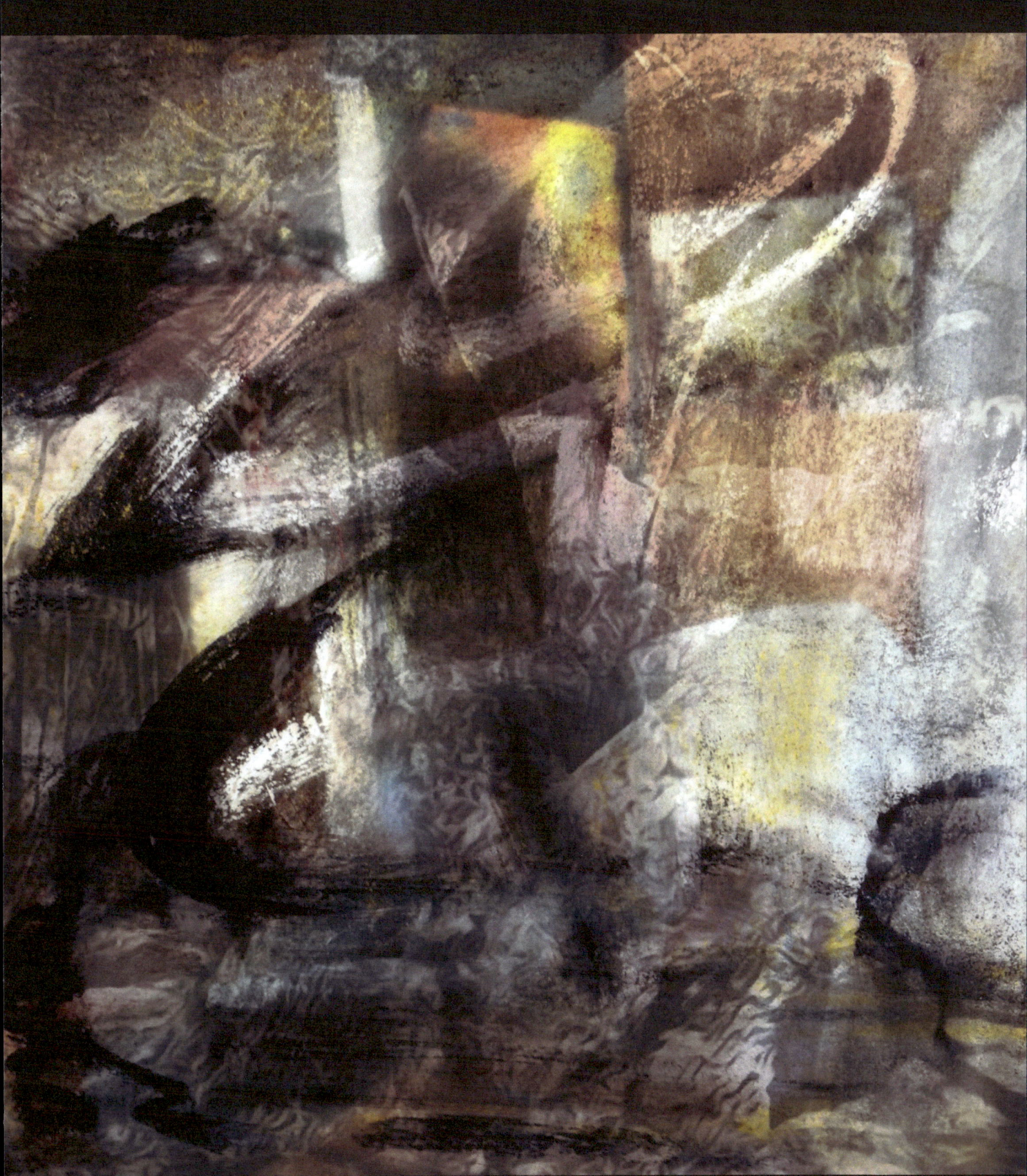

Running from Grief

"As for me, tears dim my vision"

Y. Katznelson - Poet and Playwright
Murdered in Auschwitz in 1944

"Charles tells me the details of his separation from his parents and their arrest: 'I was so distraught that I didn't know how to cry anymore.'"

Helene Berr
1921-1945; Died in Bergen-Belisen concentration camp

Jewish men, women and children hunted down across Europe tearless; they have abandoned grief; it is too heavy; they cannot carry it any more. Life must be lived now without tears. Yet tears still exist, unwept over their destroyed lives, homes, hopes and hearts. Where did they hold their tears? Have they left them behind in attics and barns, in holes dug out in the earth, small places to hide, brief shelters from the Nazi's unrelenting hunt? Have they forgotten how to cry? Do their tears scorch the earth, leaving trails of grief, anguish and disbelief? Did they have to run from grief to survive? Tears could dim visions; hold one in a past composed of family meals, shared joys of Holy Days; the ability to work and live and play and be the Jews of Europe. To visit a place of the mind and heart that no longer exists must not be allowed. But it is our time now; grief time. We who stand here; we can cry and pour out our tears of anger and sorrow at your destruction. We have six million tears and they create a flood of our determination to not run from our grief, but to carry it with yours. We vow here and now to stand up in grief time to reclaim your lives; to tell your stories. To celebrate who you were; how you lived; who you might have been and to those of you who survived, we shout out your stories. In grief time, we pause to remember. Our promise never to forget is not an idle one; it is a sacred vow; the air we breathe; the life we live.

Rabbi Stephanie S. Aaron

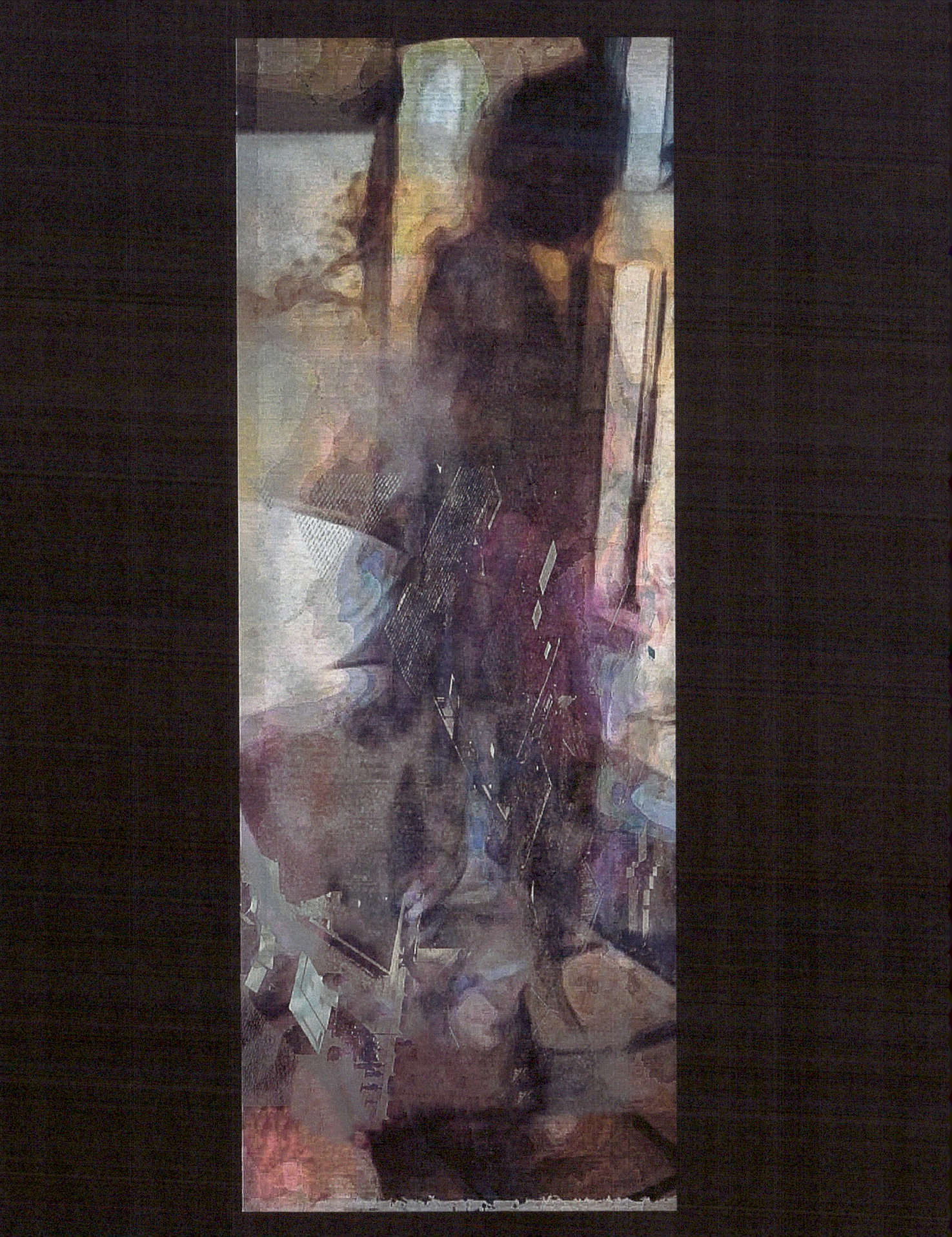

A Dream

Their dream was to be free. This is the dream that helped to keep their spirits up and kept them alive.

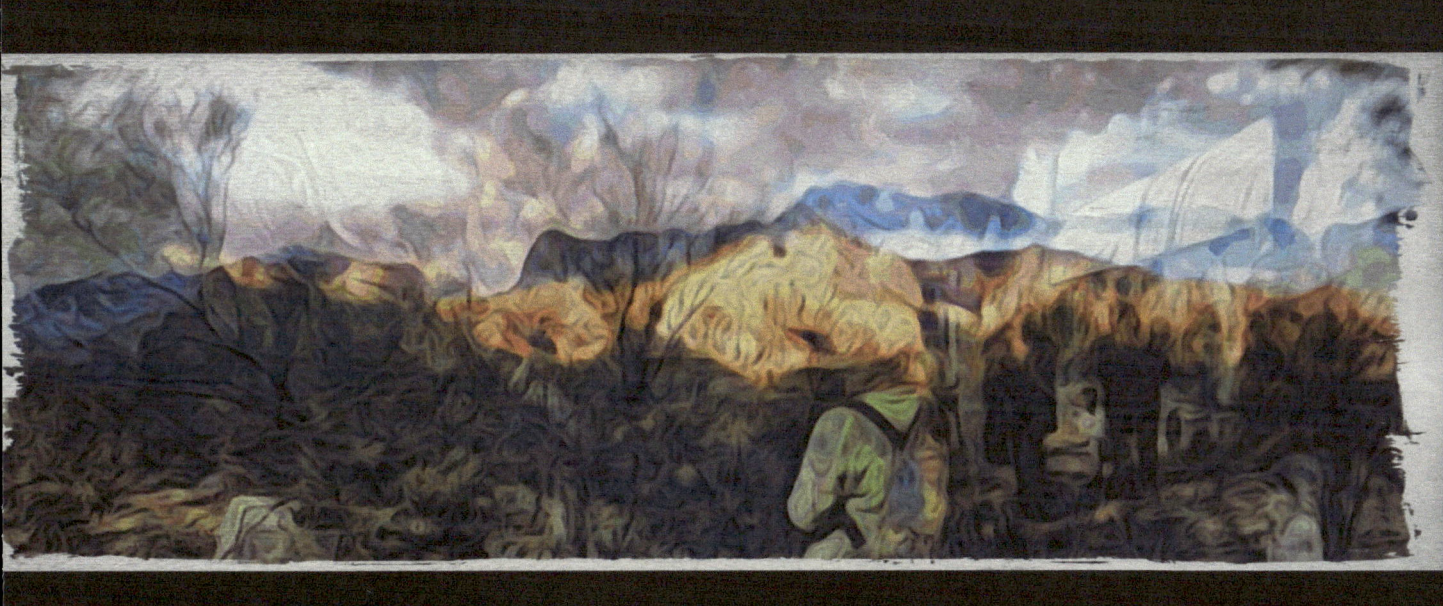

Defiant

Being locked up in a camp was in itself a horrific experience. Escape at all costs from the sadism of the Gestapo was necessary to save his sanity and his family's life. Joining the Partisans had to become a reality. There was no choice. Fight back or be killed. At this time his father and mother had been shot in the woods. Sol's only thought was to get his family to a safe place.

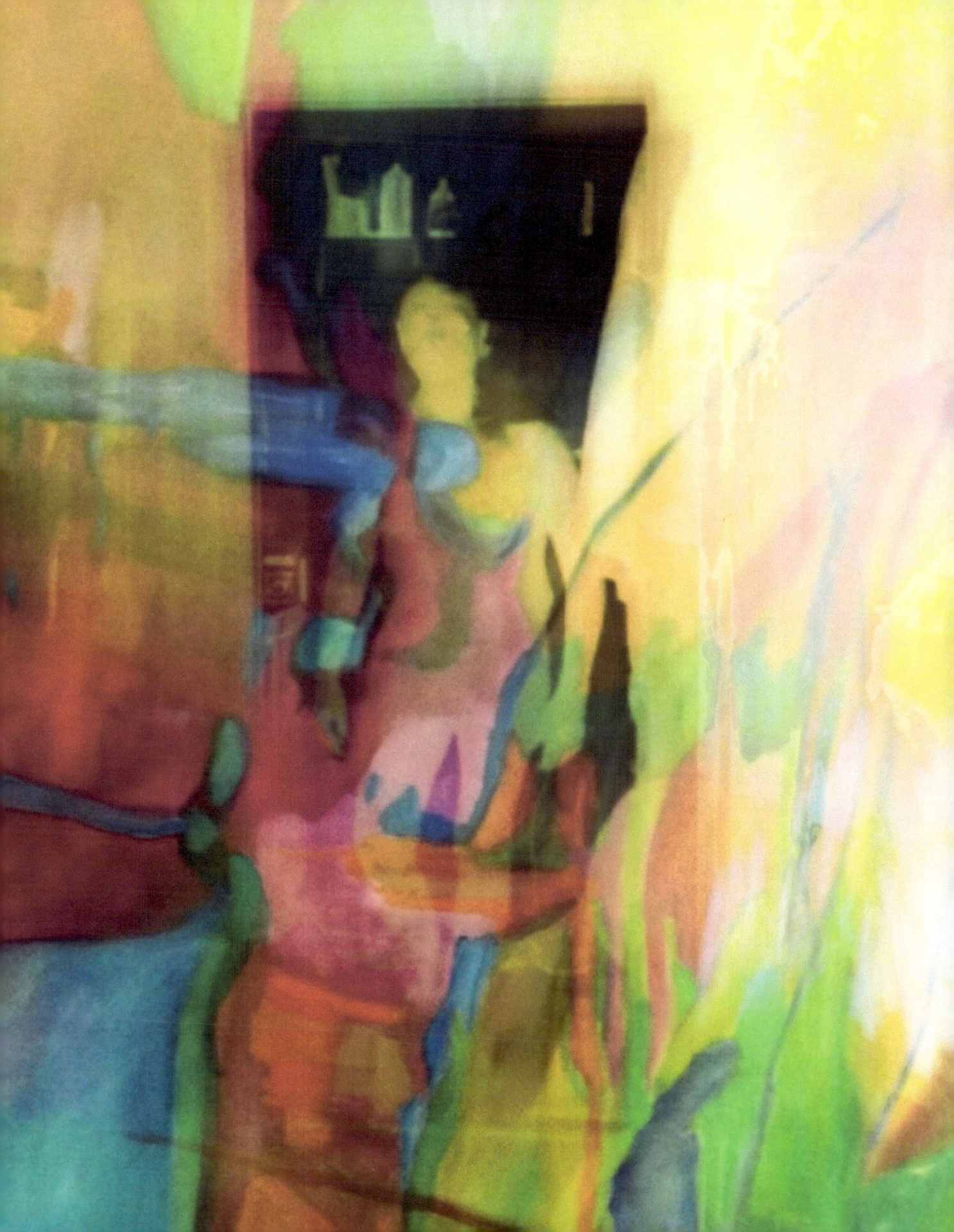

Kantarovich Building
July 19, 1943

Mass killings began in the ghetto of Glubokoye. People were running for their lives. My mother and father ran to the Kantarovich building which was rumored to have a bomb shelter. Only six remained in hiding and were the only survivors of 20,000 murdered in the brutal massacre of the town of Glubokoye that day.

Excerpt from Sol's Memoirs

"They took up positions outside the ghetto and opened up with their artillery and machine-guns and mortars, subjecting the ghetto to a horrendous crossfire which swept every street and house within the fence. Fires broke out all around and shells plowed up the streets and crashed into frail houses, almost obliterating them. In the midst of all this, I grabbed my brother Aaron by the hand, took my baby son Efryim in my arms and, with Luba behind me, started to run toward the barbed-wire."

"As the heavy firing continued, people were being cut down all around us, as they milled in panic within the enclosure. My baby son received a bullet in the left cheek, as I held him, his right cheek resting against mine. He died in my arms, his blood all over my clothes. Had he not been there, the bullet that killed him would have killed me. My younger brother Aaron received a bullet in the chest and died on the spot."

"I found myself all alone. My baby son and younger brother were both dead, killed before my eyes. I was certain that Luba had also met her death."

"Without knowing why, I decided to try and make a run for the Kantarovich building, and the bomb shelter. Running across the main street, still being swept by artillery and mortar fire, I suddenly saw Luba trying to cross main street. To this day I am still amazed at how we escaped the crossfire and made it out alive."

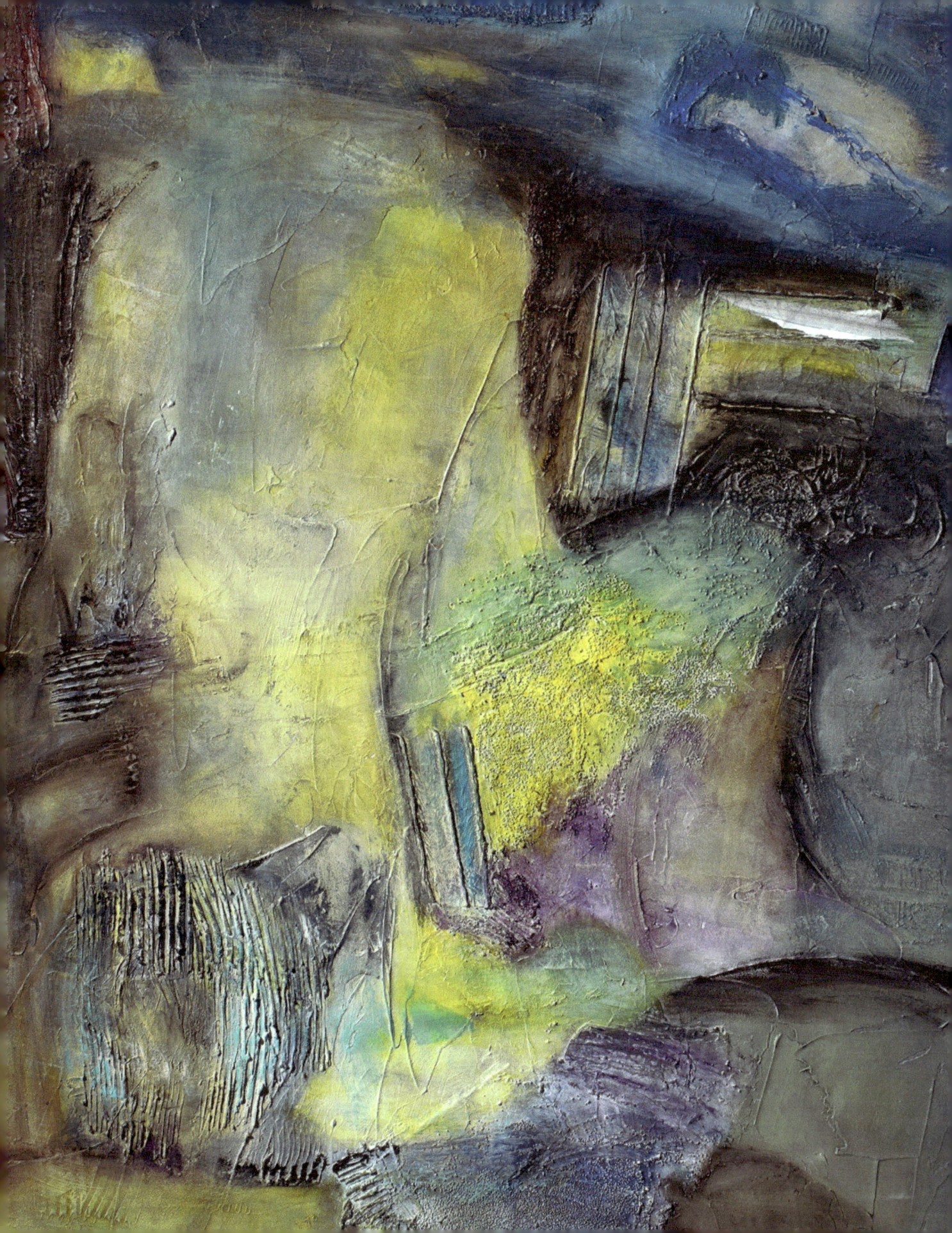

The Mission
July 27, 1943

Because he had survived the devastation of Glubokoye, my father's first mission with the Partisan army was a test of loyalty.

Excerpt from Sol's Memoirs

"First I would not be permitted to carry firearms of any kind. Second, when we reached the target area, I would have to precede the main body by at least one hundred and fifty feet; that when we reached the exact spot to be destroyed, I was to remain there alone for a least ten minutes. If my presence wasn't detected, I was to return to the main body, waiting in the woods behind me. Then I was to lead them back to the target. They would then plant the dynamite, timing the charge for thirty minutes. After the charge was planted I was to stay behind ten minutes, to give them a chance to get away. The reason for this was simple. If I turned out to be a traitor, that extra ten minutes would give them a chance to kill me, and get away themselves."

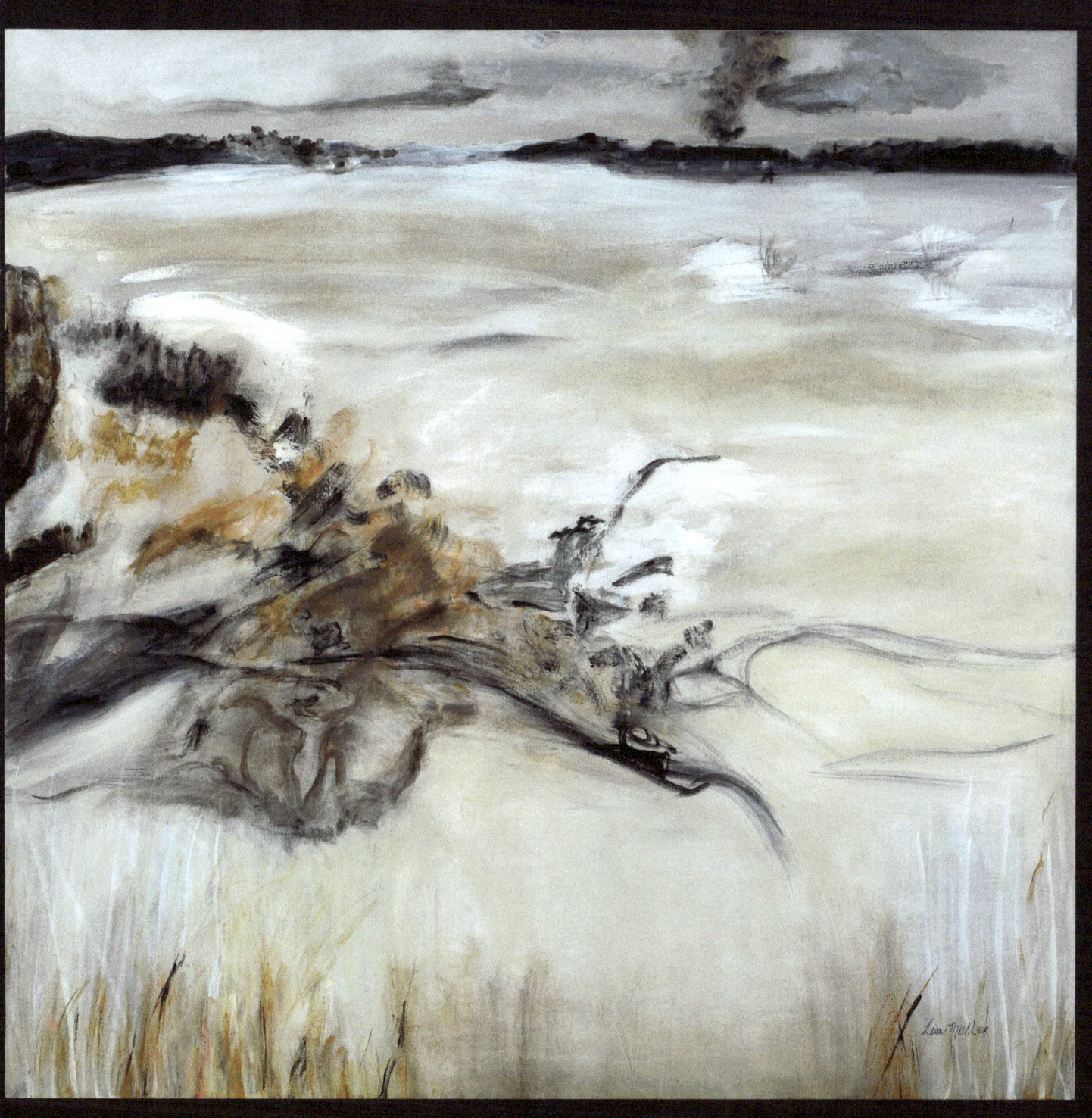

Tank
Excerpt from Sol's Memoirs

"On the day before Christmas, December 24, 1944, the big advance on Koeningsburg, Germany began. The battle was vicious, and our brigade sustained thousands of casualties in men and equipment. Wrecked and burning tanks were strewn all over the battlefields by the hundreds, and on January 6th, 1945, in the midst of heavy action, Major Lipsitz' lead tank received a direct hit. I was the first to climb out of the tank, which caught on fire. Two more men, with their pack radio, jumped out as the tank became engulfed in heavy smoke. I crawled to the top of the tank and looked inside to see what had happened to Major Lipsitz. Standing on top of the tank, I reached into the turret with my right arm, and called to Major Lipsitz. He answered in a weak voice that there was no use trying to save him, that he was hurt too badly to be moved. He ordered me to contact the second lead tank and his chief of staff, Major Serkin, and in his name, order him to keep on the offensive, 'Pierod! Pierod! Pierod!' izn Russian, meaning 'Forward! — no matter the cost' and then radio brigade headquarters for reinforcements and air cover as quickly as possible.

As he gave me these instructions, his voice faded away, and I knew he was dead. The tank consumed itself in flames. I was about to withdraw my arm from the turret, when the heavy hatch-cover suddenly slammed down on my arm catching it between the hatch-cover and rim of the turret. I thought my arm had been severed, and I began to yell for help. The two men who had jumped out of the tank with me ran to our flaming tank. They raised the hatch-cover which released my arm, smashed, bleeding and dangling from my shoulder like a pendulum.

I don't remember feeling anything at the time. All I could remember was that I needed to order my men to contact the second lead tank and the chief of staff, Major Serkin. In the name of Major Lipsitz, they were to advance no matter the cost. After the first message was transmitted to Major Serkin, I ordered my men to relay another message to brigade headquarters, to request urgent reinforcements and air cover. At the same time, the men begged me to lie still until they could locate the medics to carry me to a field hospital. I was losing a lot of blood, and my back had swollen to twice its size. I told them to carry out their orders and not to bother about me. After the messages were sent, I passed out."

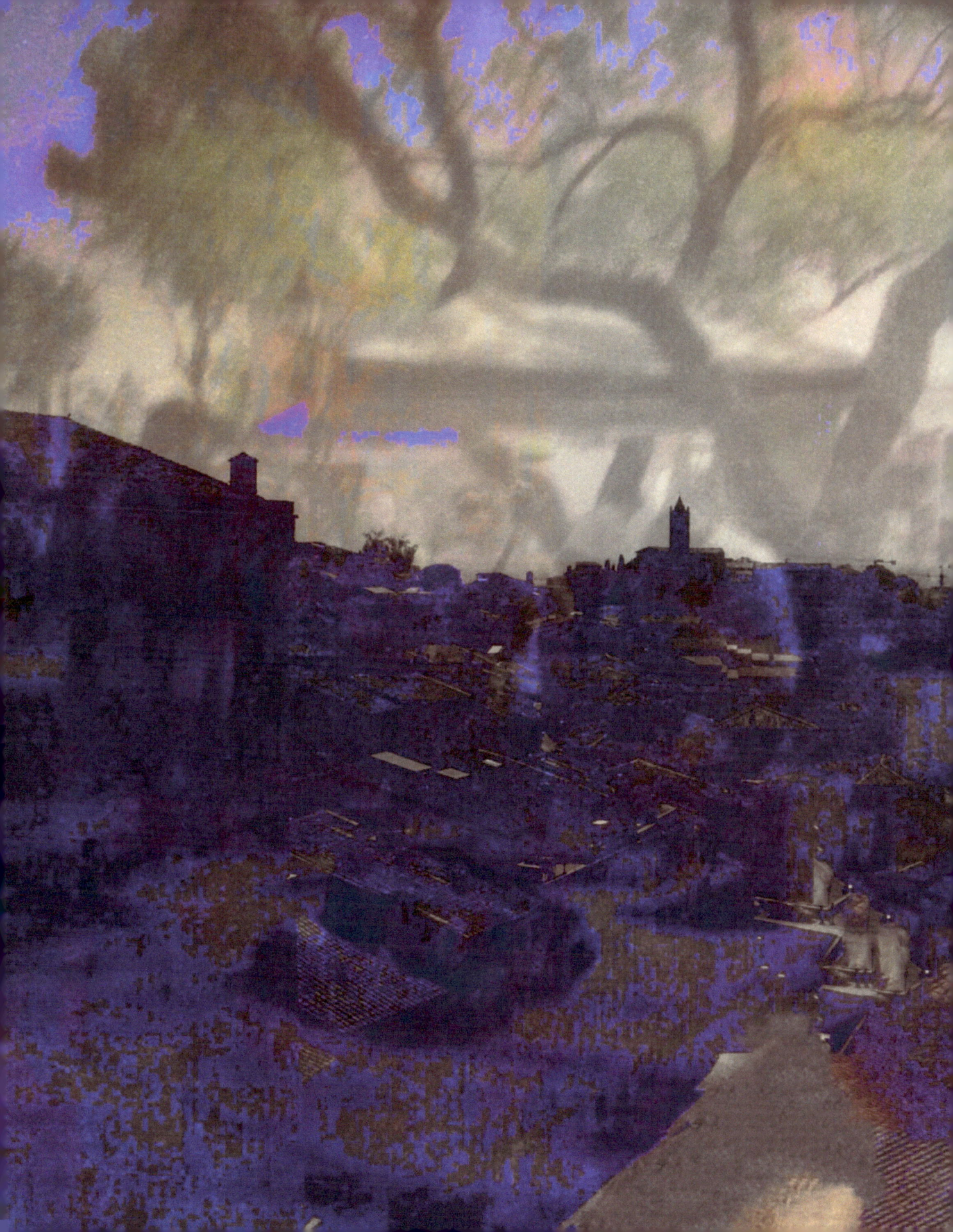

Red

"The prophet Job cried out, "Earth do not cover my blood; let there be no resting place for my outcry!" All over Europe, on riverbanks, in fields, on pathways through the countryside; all over Europe, their blood has been 'covered over'; on city streets, in their houses where the grandchildren of their neighbors' now live, in the places where synagogues once stood; all over Europe, their blood has been covered over. On the railway tracks that traverse Europe, in the universities and the hospitals, the libraries and the cafes, all over Europe, their blood has been covered over. I want to uncover their blood. I want to walk into synagogues that have been turned into libraries and museums and I want to uncover their blood by calling out the names of every Jew who lived in those towns, who prayed in those synagogues. I will uncover their blood with our prayers, chanted fiercely, passionately; no longer covered over by the silence of collusion. I will uncover their blood by insisting on remembrance of their lives. Who were these six million Jews? What were their names; what were their dreams, plans and hopes? Europe: uncover their blood! Do not just erect memorials and museums to the Shoah; every person must become the memorials; must behave as though they have inscribed the words and teachings upon their hearts. Europe: uncover their blood; remove antisemitism, racism, prejudice, bigotry, and hatred from your lives and the lives of your children. 'All over Europe, their blood has been covered over.'

Rabbi Stephanie S. Aaron

After seeing my painting titled "Red", Rabbi Aaron was reminded of the diary written by the young man, Moshe Flinker (1926-1944), who was murdered in the Shoah. She was then inspired to write the prose above.

Transition Point

The cold, the gray, dark air, the starkness of our aloneness; we were so alone, isolated by the enormity of their hatred. Would we dissolve into the gray bleakness of our solitude; would we become hopeless people who could not see a way forward? We struggled to overcome the gray depths, the hunger, the thirst, the unknowns of: where are our families; does anyone still live? We whispered Moses' words to Joshua, "Chazak ve'ematz; be strong and have good courage." We pulled one another forward toward the lights of life; tikvah, we said, tikvah, hope; we are a people of hope. We will fight; we will wrestle with darkness; we know its dangers. We will not despair. We will find our way forward into the light of tikvah.

Rabbi Stephanie S. Aaron

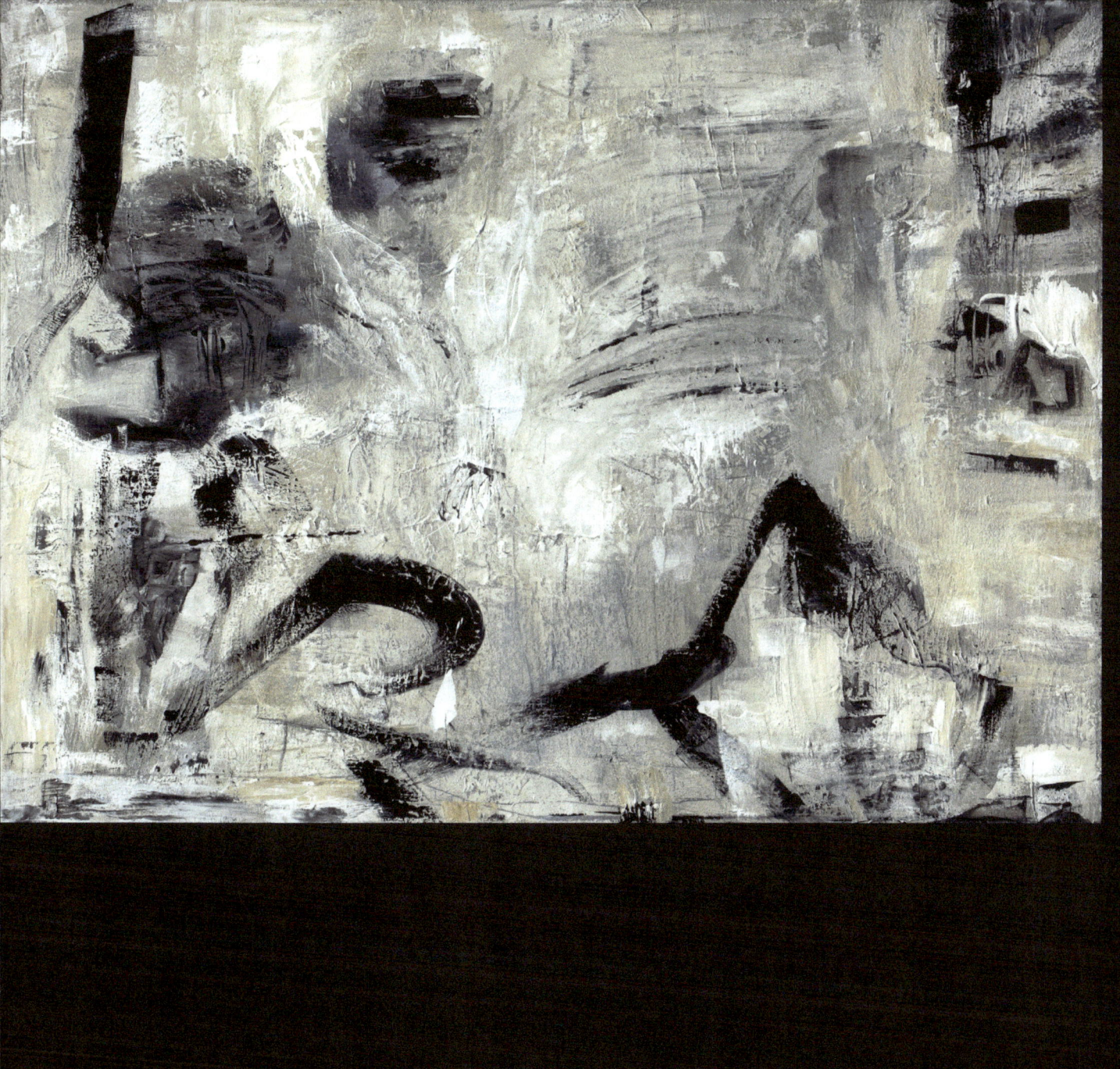

Camouflage

Fighting with the Partisans.

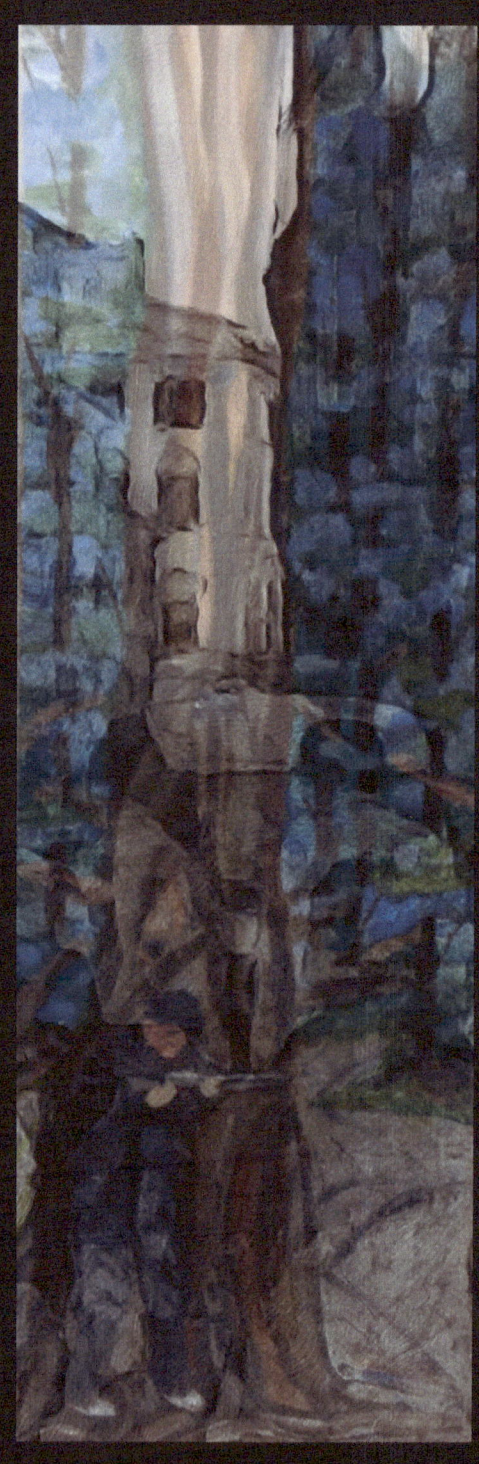

Winter in Germany

This winter of horror (1942) was one of the coldest winters recorded.

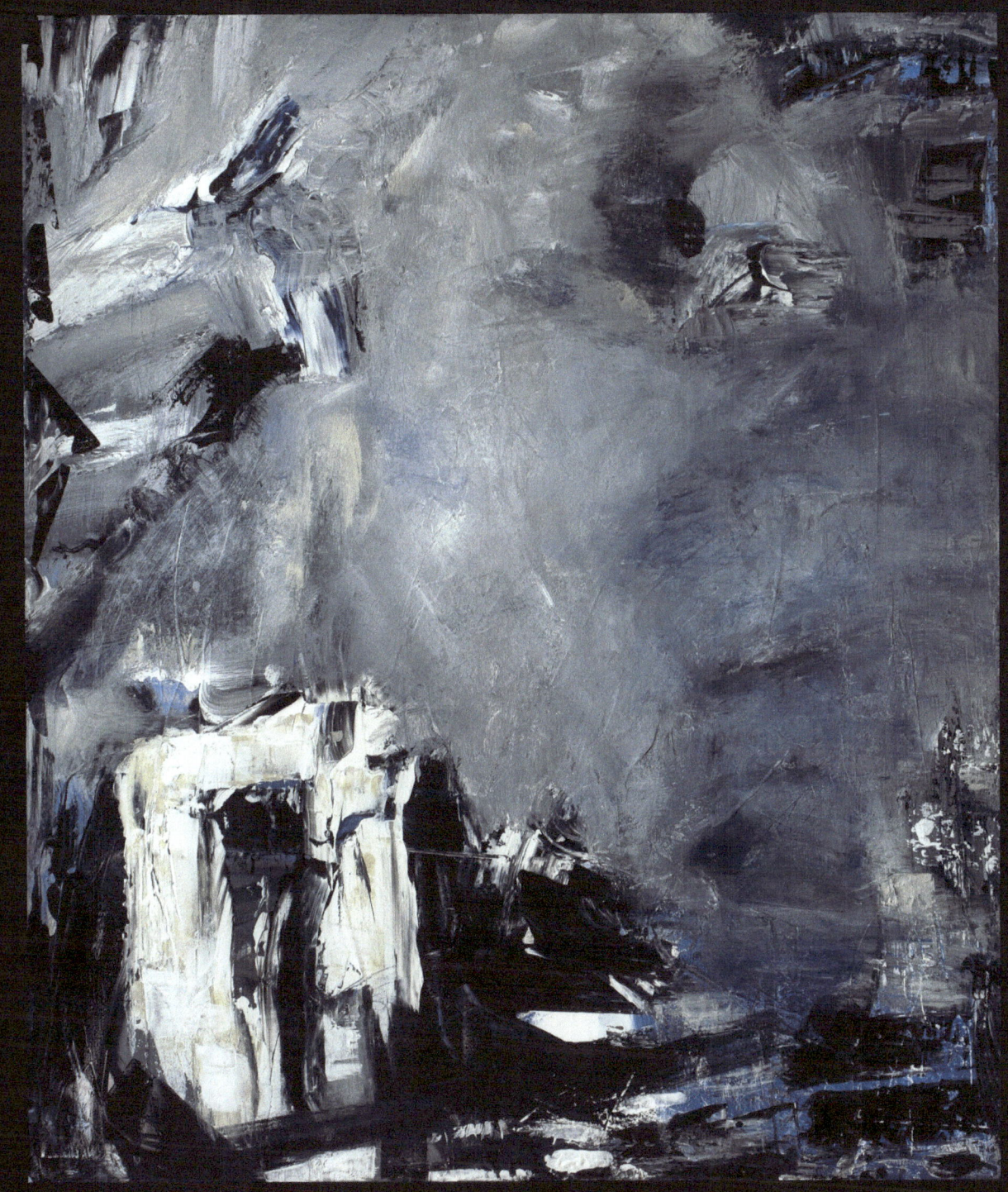

Raven

I see the raven symbolizing mysticism, spirituality and hope. It is often referenced in the Bible (Kings:17.4 -6).

God told Elijah to go into the wilderness and live there alone by the side of a small brook. Elijah went to the brook where there was plenty of water to drink but no food to keep him from starving. God did not abandon his servant. He sent ravens to carry food to Elijah. "The ravens brought him bread and meat in the evening; and he drank of the brook." It is interpreted that Elijah was fed in this way for as much as a year. This is why I chose the image of the raven, for it represents hope and sustenance.

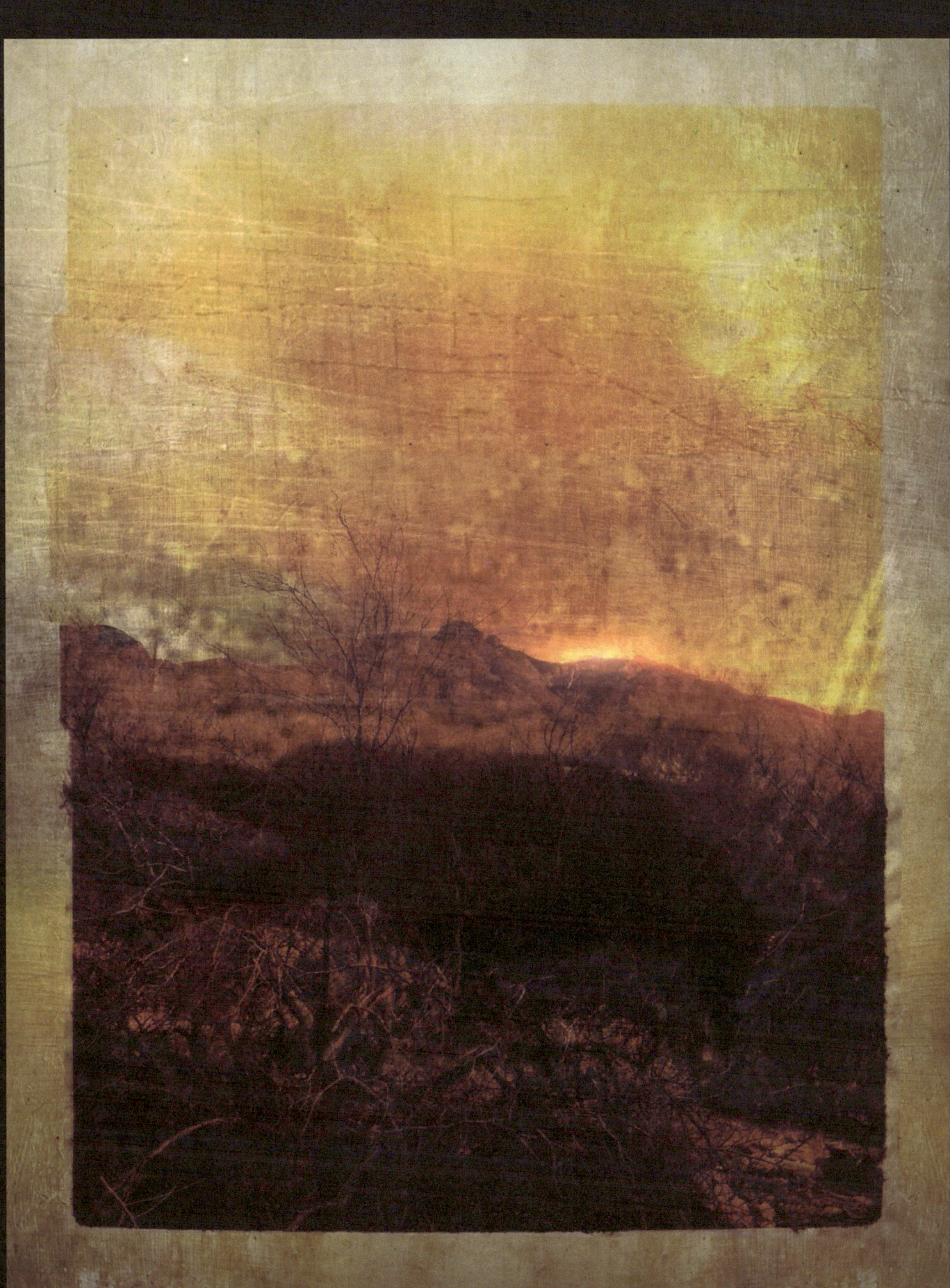

Renewal

Painting the sky yellow; I wonder what we would use for our yellow, what strand of yellow would it be? The golden yellow flecks that sparkle in the brown of your eyes, making the brown light up hazel? Would it be that yellow? Or the dazzle of a daffodil bursting out of the earth to announce spring and life and love? Where would we find the yellow of an egg yolk, round with promise, bright with nourishment? Perhaps we would paint the sky shiny challah yellow, a yellow braided with the torment of our yearning and our desolation. What is Jew-yellow? The color of our voices rising up to scream, "Enough, enough, enough!" Is it the glimmer of gold burning at the edge of blue in a Shabbas candle? Is Jew-yellow the color of hope?

Rabbi Stephanie S. Aaron

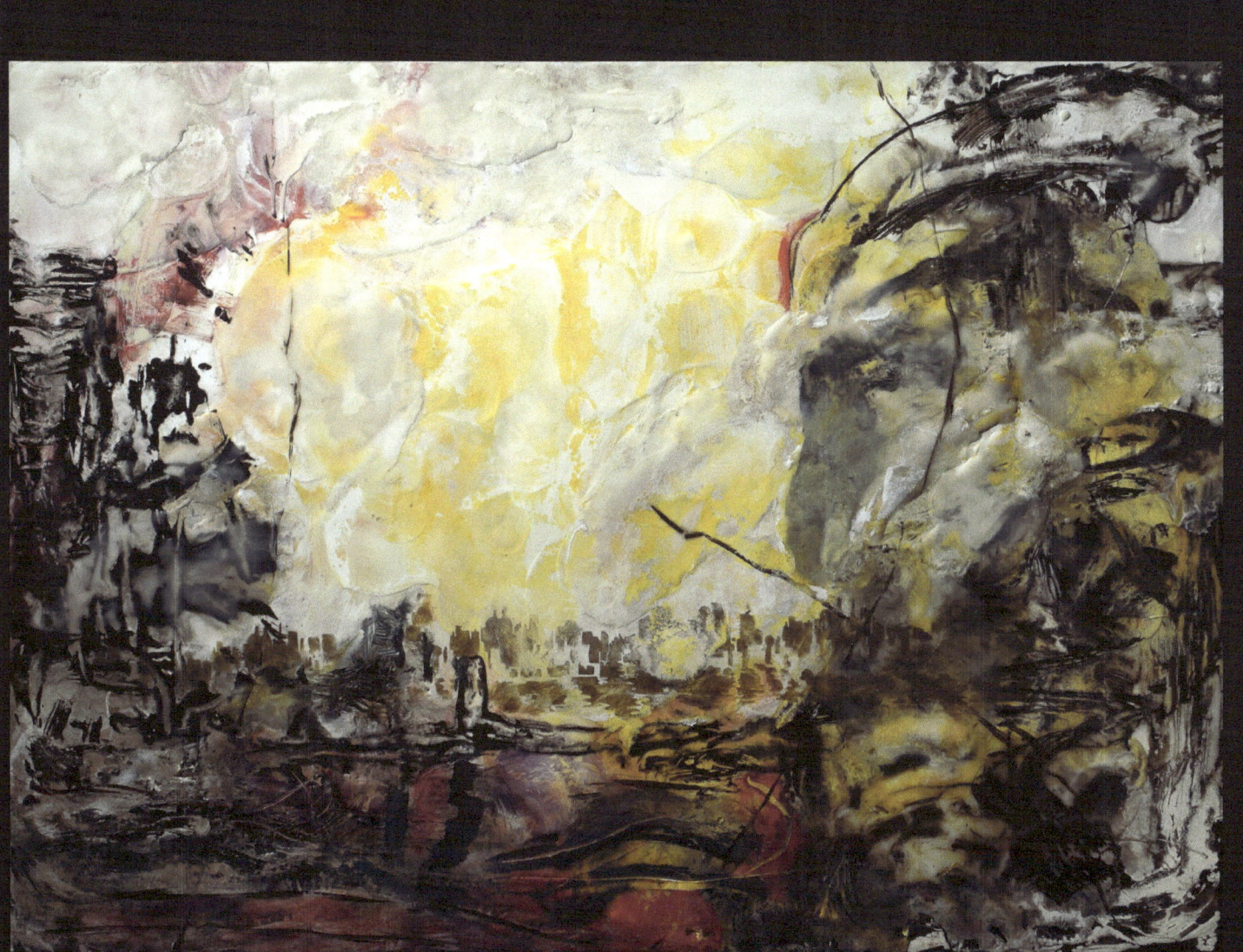

Moving Into the Light

There is even dancing, although the stomach is empty. It is almost a mitzvah to dance. The more one dances, the more it is a sign of his belief in the 'eternity of Israel'. Every dance is a protest against our oppressors.

Chaim A. Kaplan, Warsaw Ghetto
Died in Treblinka death camp

Dance with me although my stomach is empty; my head is dizzy with hunger. Our waltz drags; we stagger in the mitzvah of this dance. How did you do it, Chaim Kaplan? You sorted out the steps of a dance from the overwhelming despair and horror of that time, that place. You who also wrote, "If it were said the sun has darkened for us at noon, it would be true. We will rot within the narrow streets and crooked lanes in which tens of thousands of people wander, idle and full of despair". You astound me with your 'proof of life'; you brought up hope and danced with her, a whirl of dissent, a claim on life and beauty with loving lines of a dance.

Rabbi Stephanie S. Aaron

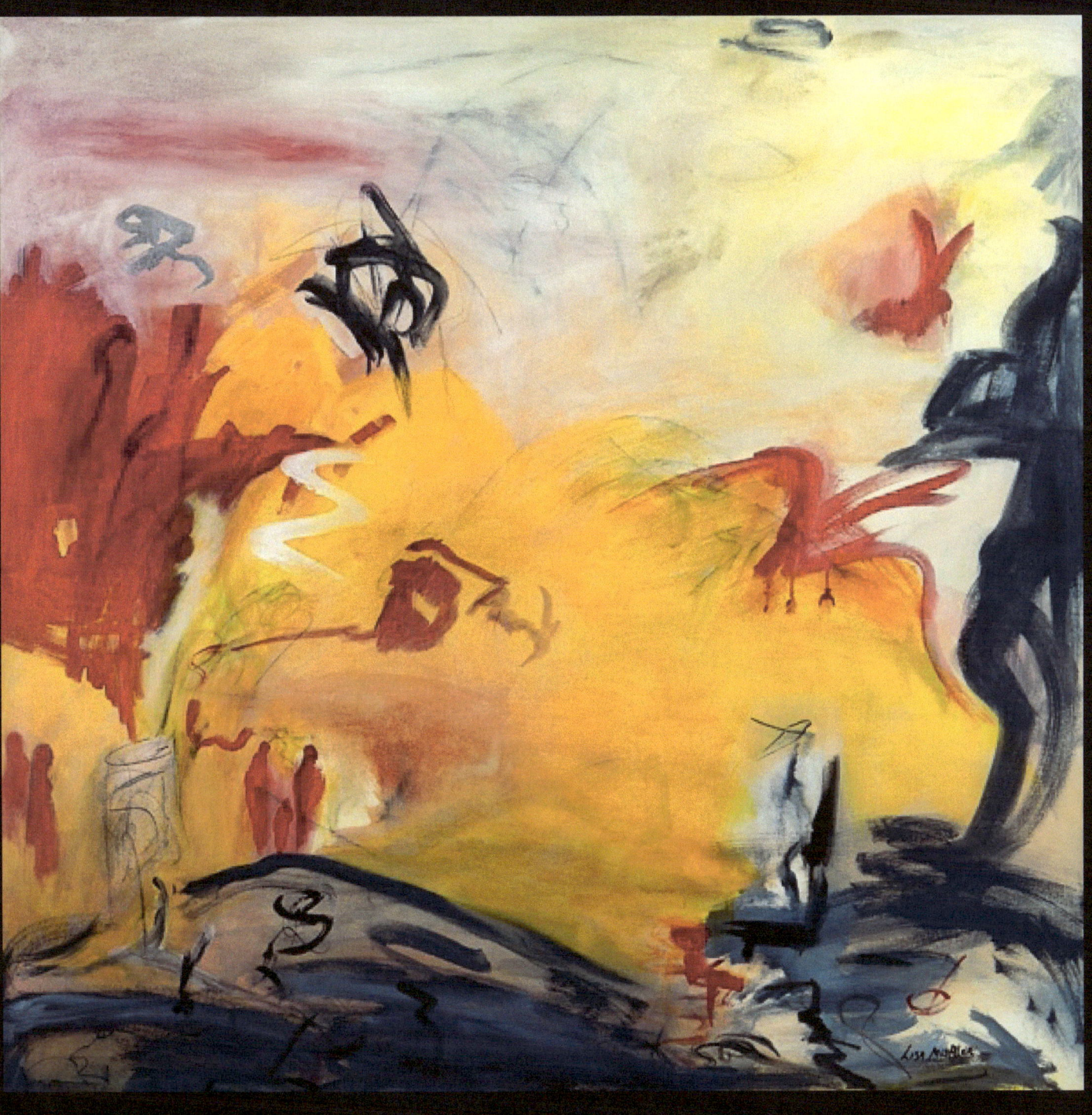

My Father's Legacy

The indomitable spirit of Sol and Luba is their legacy. They did not succumb to the horrors of what they experienced during the war years, the anguish of their personal losses or the attempts to annihilate their cultural heritage and religion.

My father always had the dream of owning a gentleman's ranch. Now his granddaughter Stephanie is living that dream.

I believe my father would have appreciated Elton John's "Live Like Horses", lyrics by Bernie Taupin.

"Some day we'll live like horses
Free rein from your old iron fences.
There's more ways than one to regain your senses
Break out the stalls and we'll live like horses."

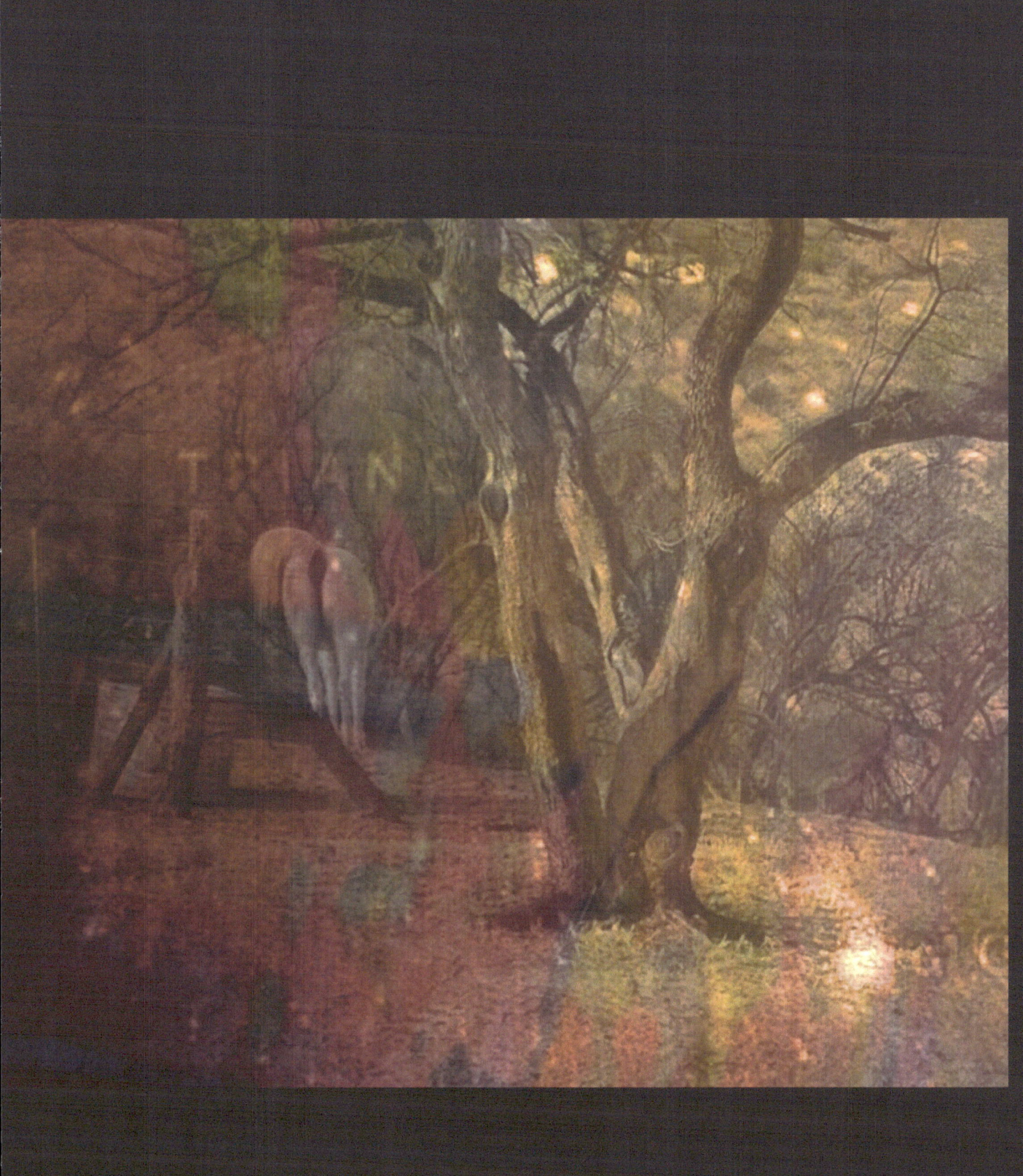

Bashert - Meant to be
March 18, 1946

It was six months after the war had ended and displaced people were looking for new beginnings. Lodz, Poland was the first center organized to help Jewish refugees from eastern Poland and Russia. My parents had been separated when my father joined the Russian army. After the war my father was headed to the United States with help from his older sister who had connections in Washington DC. My mother had decided to head to Palestine to start her new life because she felt Jews would be safe there. It was fate that they were reunited after the war when both of their trains pulled into the station in Lodz.

Exerpt from Sol's Memoirs

"On March 18th, 1946 the train approached Lodz, and pulled into the station at 3:30 in the afternoon. As I was getting off the train, another train from the east pulled into the station on the opposite platform. One could tell that the passengers were mostly refugees because of the cut of their clothes. I suddenly was attracted by a girl getting off the train walking down the platform. From her back, it looked like Luba, enough like her to make me call out, Luba! Luba! Luba! The girl stopped and looked around. It was Luba. At first she didn't recognize me and she started to walk away. Then she realized it was me and she turned around and started running toward me. We embraced and kissed each other."

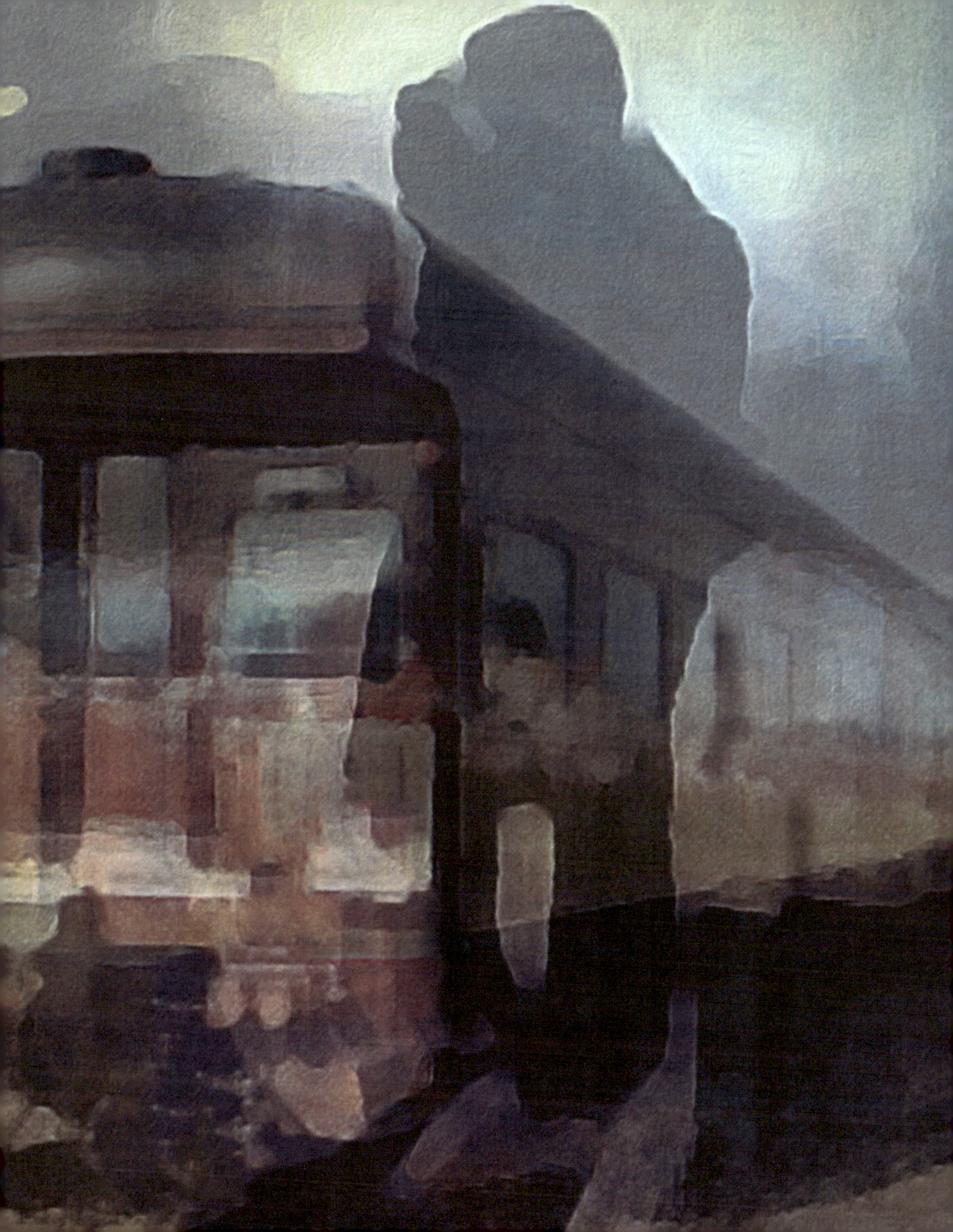

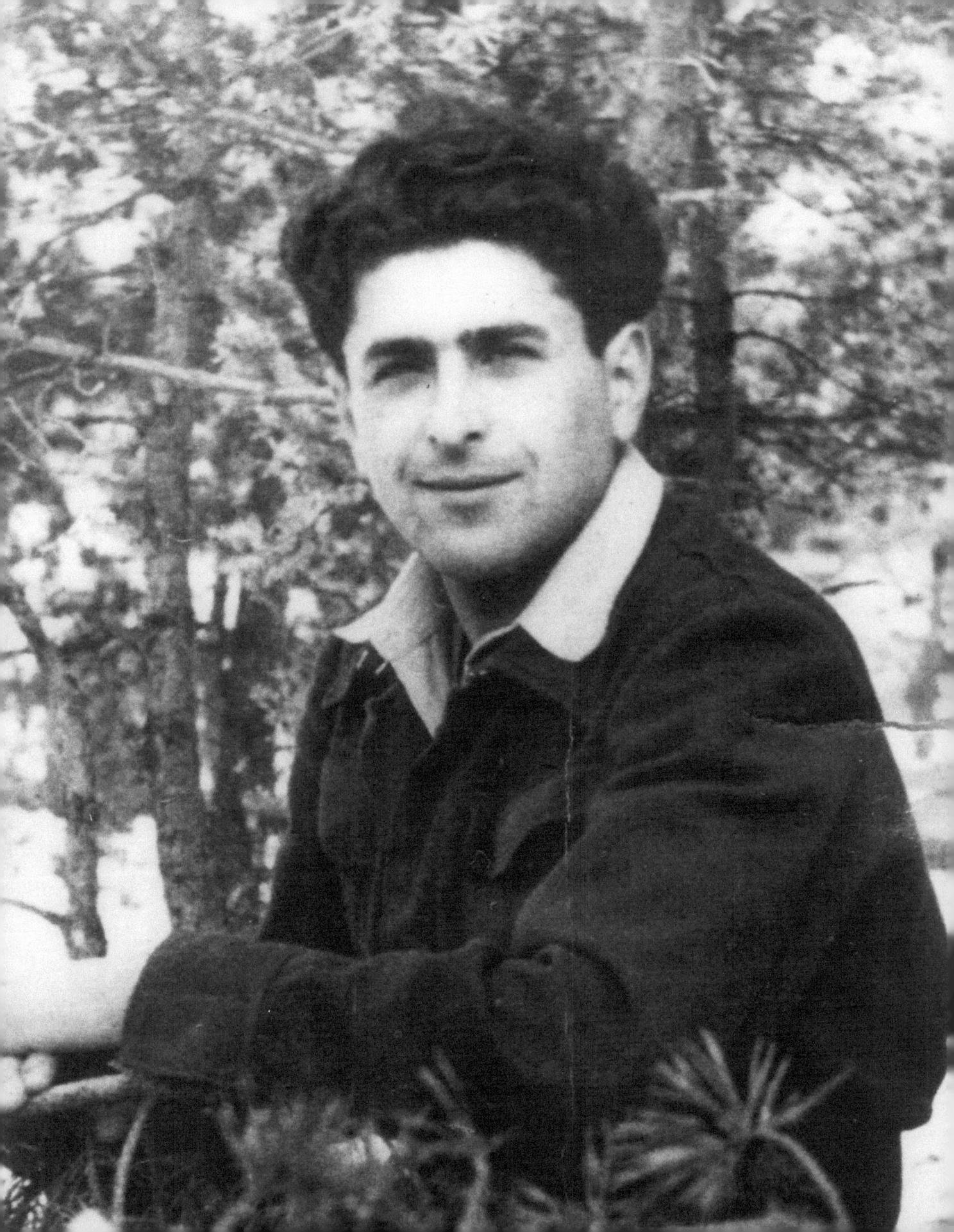

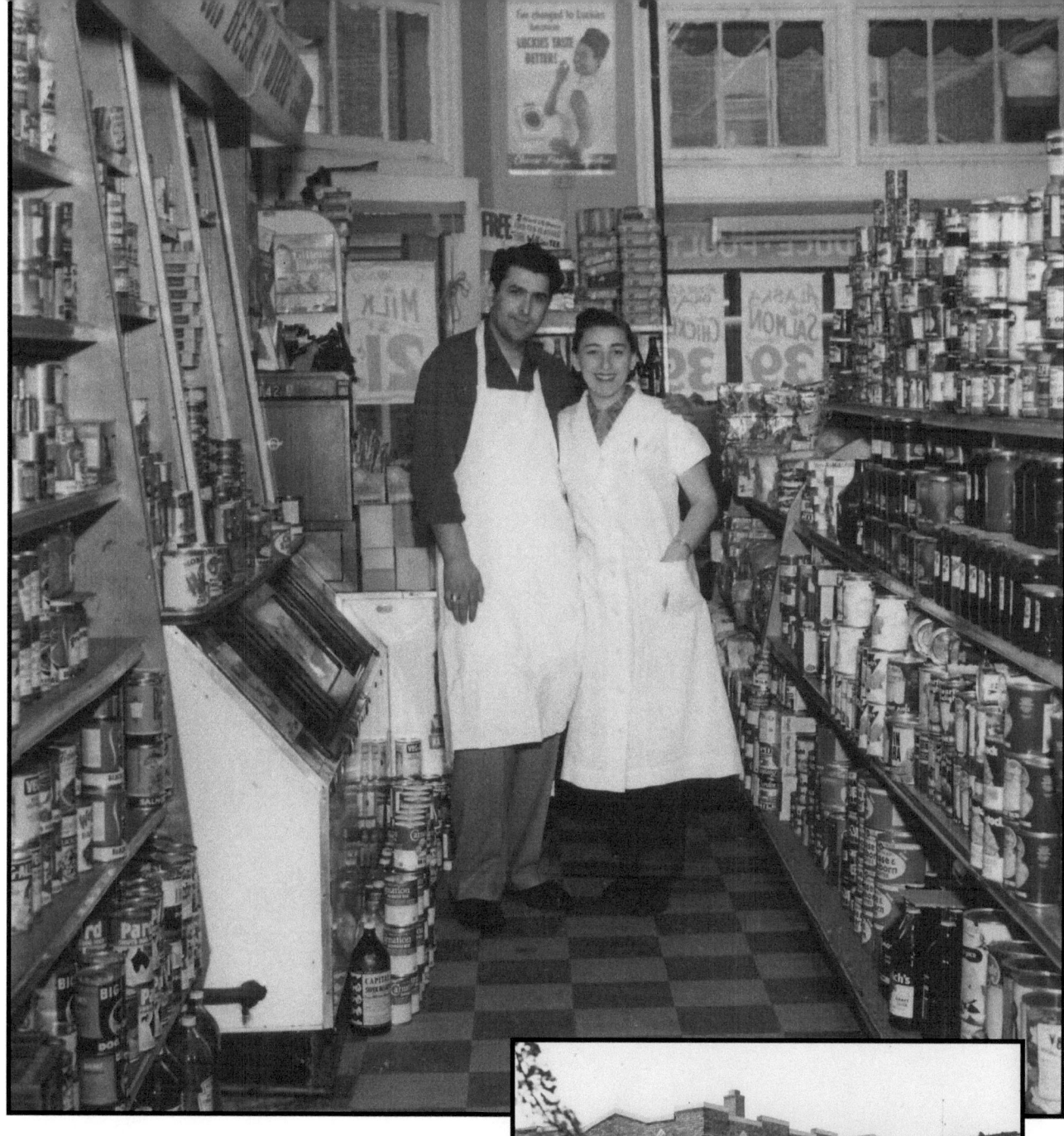

Sol and Luba's first business in
Washington D.C.

Sol Kotz at left

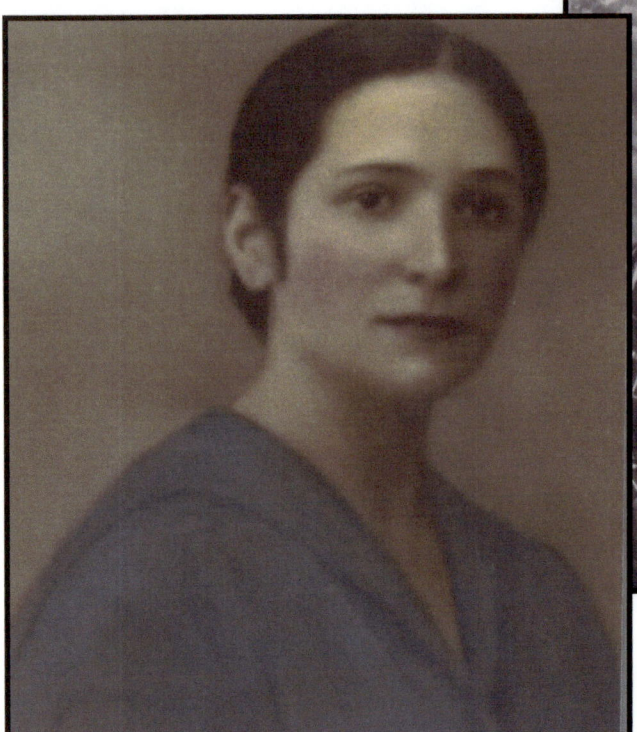

Sol's mom Ethel

Great Grandmother, Sol's mother and grandfather. Child unknown

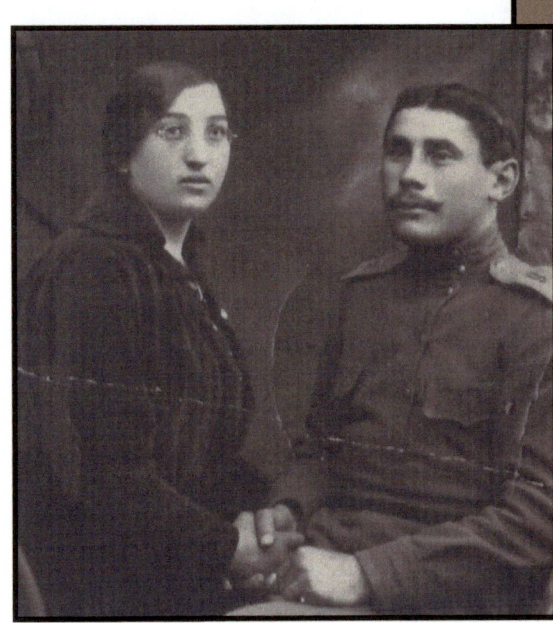

Luba's Mother and Father

Mordechai, Luba's brother

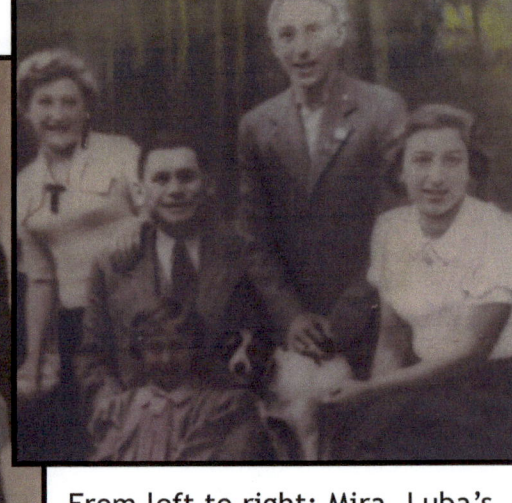

From left to right: Mira, Luba's older sister; their father and younger sister; unknown man; Luba

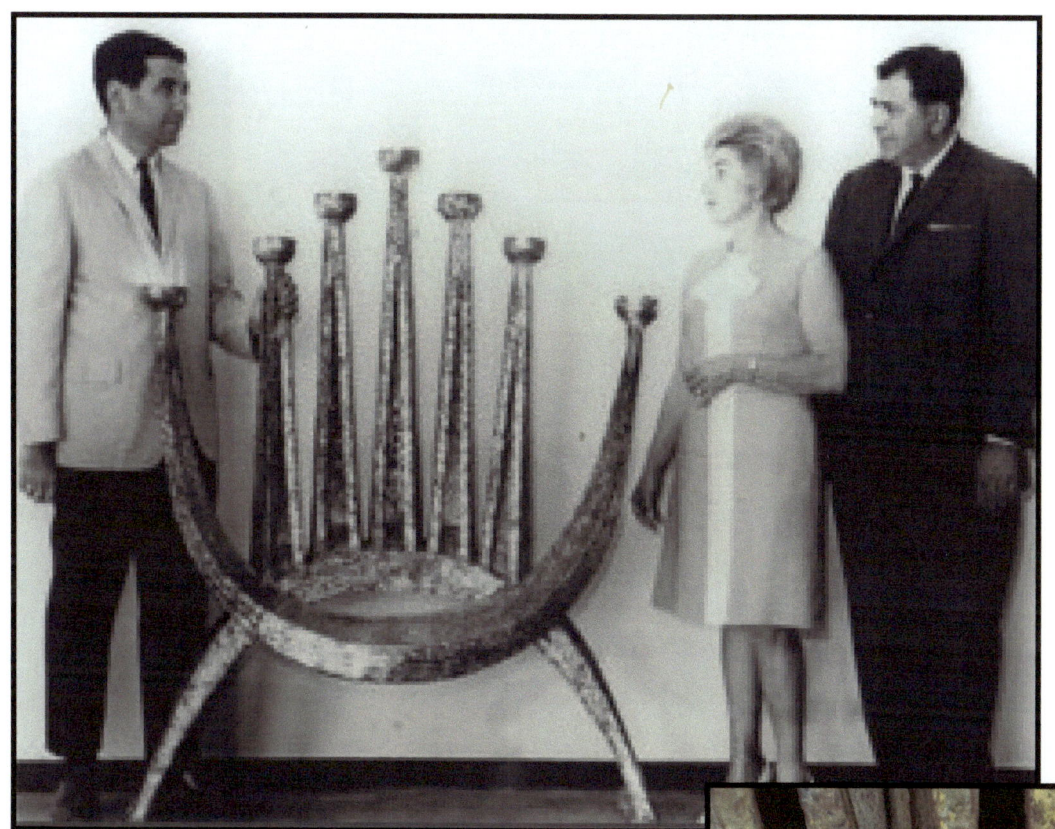

Sol Kotz was co-founder of the first Jewish synagogue in Scottsdale, Arizona. In 1967 Sol and Luba donated two Menorahs. On each Menorah is written the names of the deceased children and adults from each family

KILLED BY THE NAZIS
EFRYIM DOVID KOTZ   YEHUDAH LAYB KOTZ
ETHEL KOTZ   AHRON KOTZ
FRAYDE KOTZ   EFRYIM KOTZ
AUGUST 20, 1943

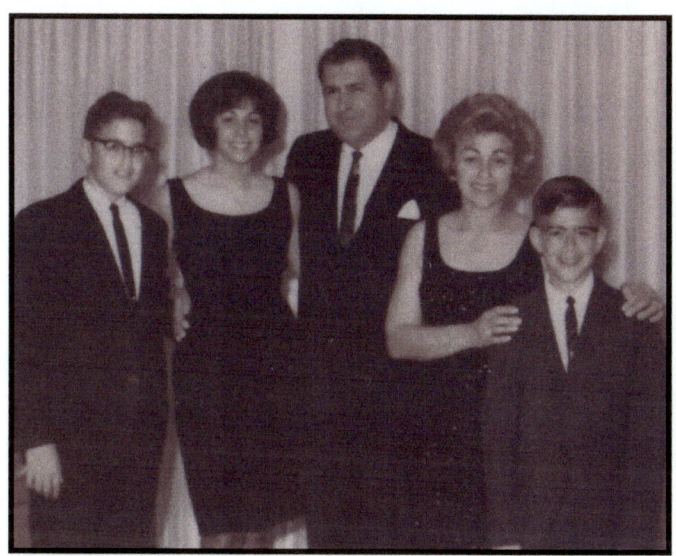

Left to right: Sheldon, me, Sol, Luba and Larry. Picture taken in 1960

47

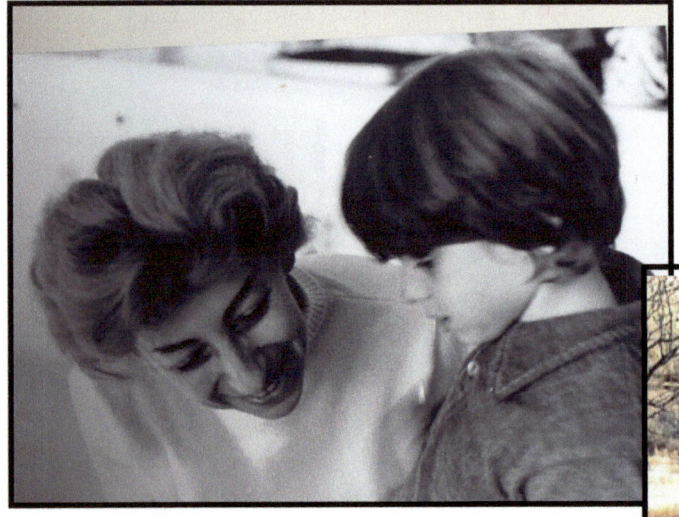

Luba with her first grandson, Sean

Luba and Sol's granddaughter,
Stephanie, with husband and
great-grandson

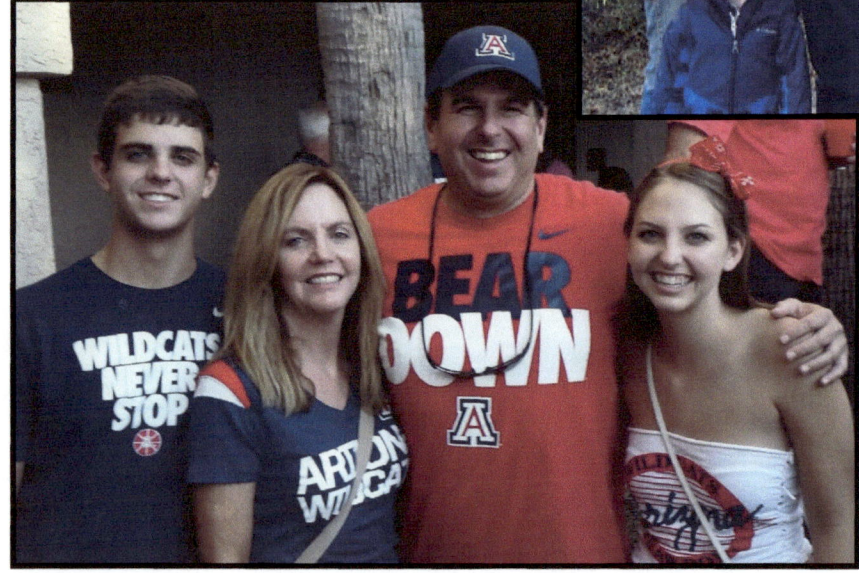

Luba and Sol's grandson, Sean with wife and great-
grandchildren Connor and Carly

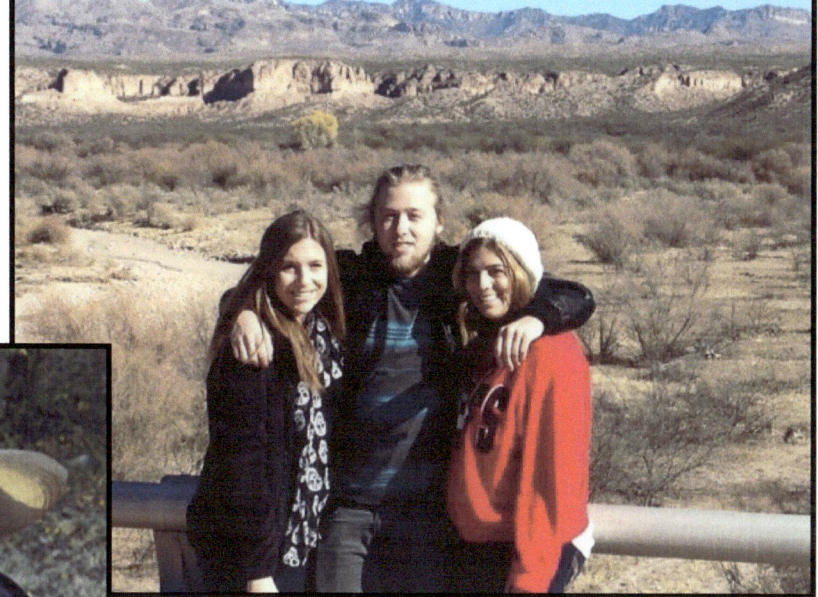

Grandchildren from their youngest son Larry:
Shelby, Jacob and Lindsey

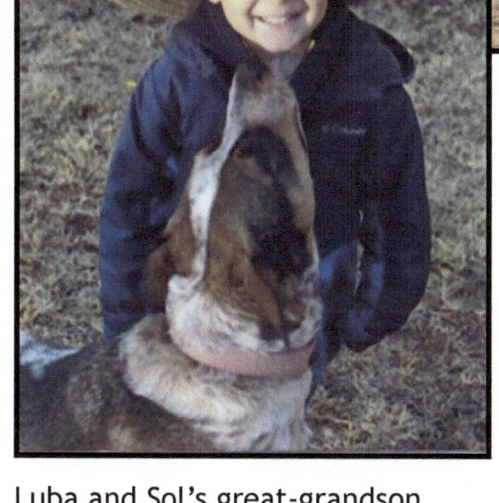

Luba and Sol's great-grandson
Paxton with his dog, Happy

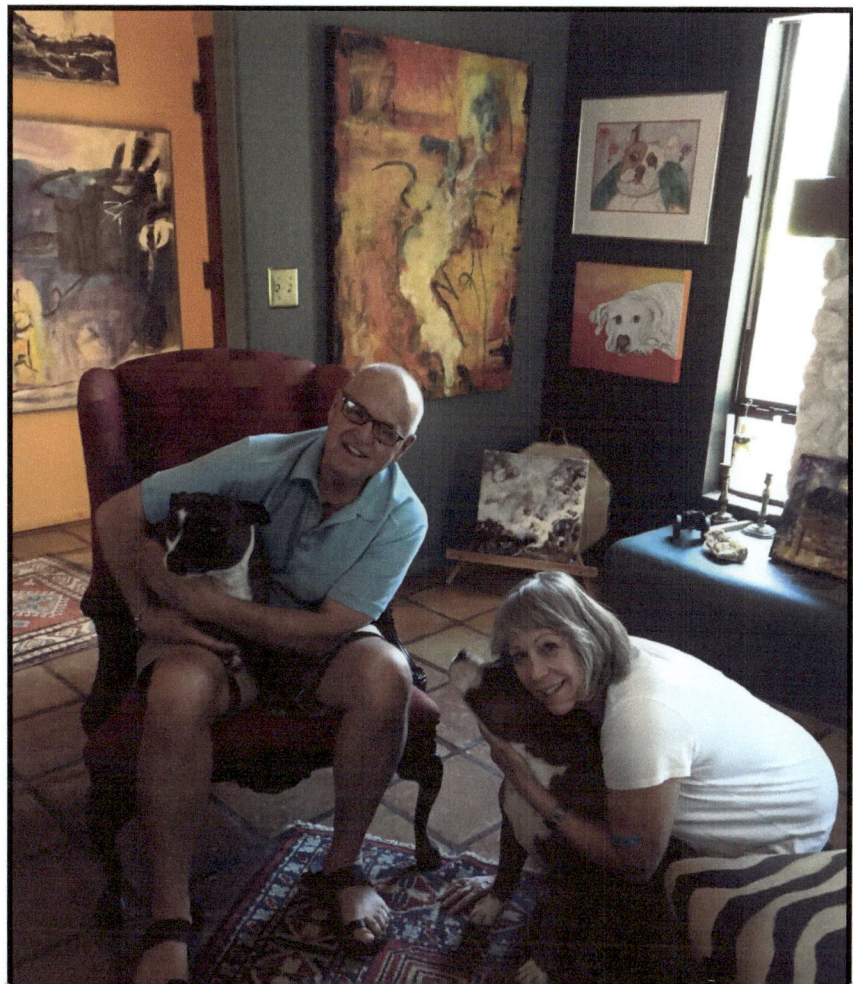

Myself and my husband
Chuck with our puppies,
Winston and Gemini

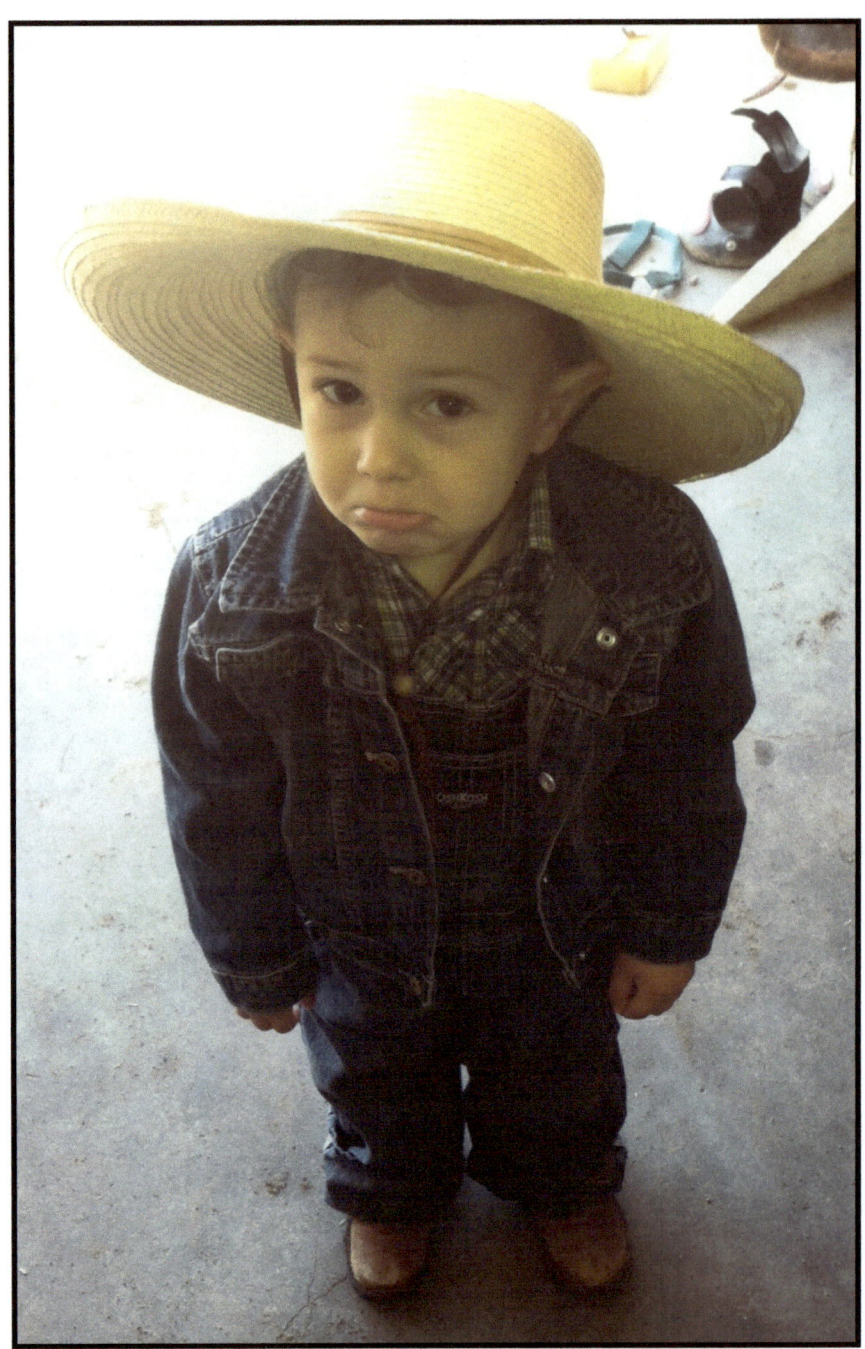

The end for now

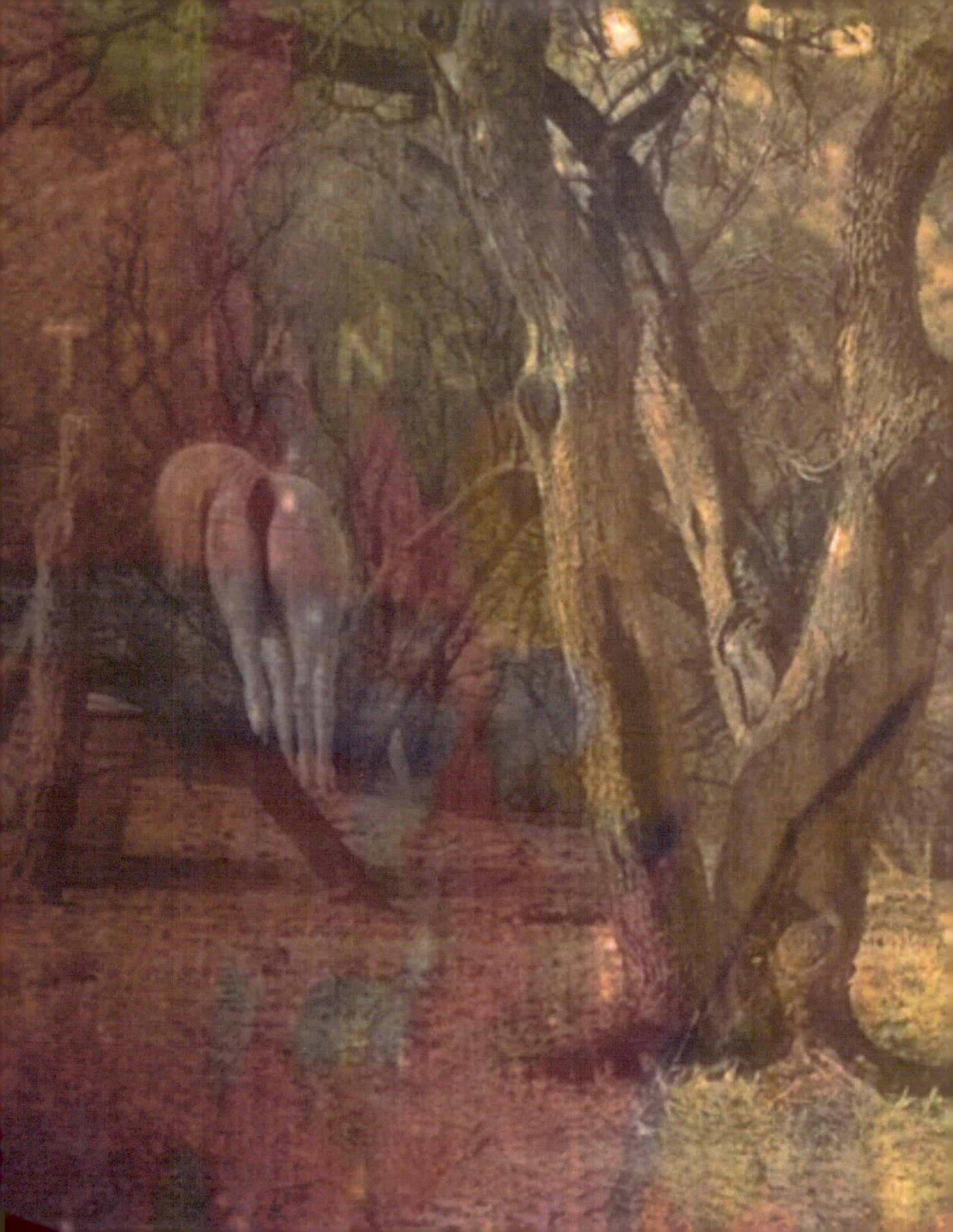

www.ingramcontent.com/pod-product-compliance
Lightning Source LLC
Chambersburg PA
CBHW042024200526
45159CB00036B/1635